Transformational Worship

"Changing Lives *through* Heartfelt Worship"

Glenn Thomas Walter
Third Edition

From my wounds will come *worship*, from my pain will come praise, from my tears will come triumph and the strength to live each day.

~ Bishop Norman L. Wagner

This project is dedicated to all who **worship** the Lord Jesus Christ in *spirit* and in **truth** for generations to come…

TABLE OF CONTENTS

FOREWORD   7

CHAPTER 1
WORSHIPPING THROUGH THE UNEXPLAINABLE

MOTHER'S UNEXPLAINABLE LOVE   11
WORSHIPPING THROUGH MOTHER'S CHALLENGE   13
WORSHIPPING THROUGH THE BATTLE   15
WORSHIPPING THROUGH TRANSITION   21
WORSHIPPING THROUGH THE UNSPEAKABLE   32
LOVE AT BIRTH: A LOVE SONG FOR CHELLY   37
READY, SET, TRANSFORMED   42
UNEXPECTEDLY UNSPEAKABLE   48
O' SPARE ME THAT I MAY RECOVER   53
HE HEALS THE BROKEN HEARTED   64
IT DOESN'T GO AWAY BUT RECOVERY
IS POSSIBLE   66
WORSHIPPING THROUGH RECONCILIATION   71
DARKEST BEFORE DAWN: IT'S NEVER TOO LATE   81
HIS EYE IS ON THE SPARROW   83
IN TRANSITION TO TRANSFORMATION   87
CLOSURE IS FOREVER   88
GOD IS IN THE DETAILS   90
WORSHIPPING THROUGH FEAR   93

CHAPTER 2
WHAT IS WORSHIP

WORSHIP   99
THE ACT OF WORSHIPPING   102
THE WORSHIPPER   103

CHAPTER 3
WORSHIPPING

WORSHIPPING IN THE SPIRIT   105
WORSHIPPING IN TRUTH   109

CHAPTER 4
THE PURPOSE OF EXISTENCE

BORN AGAIN TO WORSHIP   113
THE PRAYERFUL WORSHIPPER   115

CHAPTER 5
WORSHIPPING THROUGH CALAMITY
    JOB THE UPRIGHT OF GOD   117

CHAPTER 6
WORSHIPPING THROUGH TRANSFORMATION
    DAVID:
    THE SERVANT AFTER GOD'S OWN HEART   121

CHAPTER 7
WELCOME TO THE NEXT LEVEL
    ACCEPTING THE CALL   125
    PURSUING THE CALL   127
    PROVISIONS WITH THE PROMISE   129
    WELCOME TO THE REALM OF THE
    MIRACULOUS   136

CHAPTER 8
WORSHIPPING IN WARFARE
    THE CRAZY PRAISE   141

CHAPTER 9
TRANSITIONING TO TRANSFORMATION
    LIMINALITY: AN INTERVAL BETWEEN   151

CHAPTER 10
WORSHIP: HEALING BALM FOR YOUR SOUL
    WILT THOU BE MADE WHOLE   165
    THE WISDOM OF THE MASTER POTTER   173
    BROKEN TO BE MADE WHOLE   174
    MOLDING THE CLAY   180
    MASTER MAKE ME OVER   189

CHAPTER 11
JESUS THE ULTIMATE WORSHIPPER
    PERFORMING THE WILL OF GOD   197

REFERENCES   201

SPECIAL ACKNOWLEDGEMENTS   203

FOREWORD

By
Rev. Dr. Kevin Dudley
Professor, African-American Studies
Trinity Lutheran Seminary

I count it to be an unspeakable privilege to have crossed paths with Dr. Glenn Walter. Over the years, I have been a great admirer not only of his fruitful ministry and community accomplishments, his insightful teaching and anointed leadership, but as well, his unwavering commitment to elevating God's people to faithfulness and holiness.

I first met Dr. Walter when I happened to be an anonymous attendee at a community bible study he facilitated. I remember sitting in the congregation that evening and observing scores of parishioners young and old feverishly taking notes as he poured out of the scriptures in very meaningful and practical ways. Such is the gift behind the edifying words recorded in this timely work.

Pastors and theologians have sought always to help believers to become all that God intends and to assist the church to maturity into the fullness of Jesus Christ. Few would argue that worship is essential to the life, health, and growth of every Christ-follower. In an age where the artificial and superficial seem to dominate and consume the hearts and minds of so many, the clarion call to lives of authentic worship is absolutely necessary.

Too many people, even within communities of faith, yet remain empty, confused, ignorant, unfulfilled, impotent and unproductive due to a deficiency in their worship lives.

It is true that an ongoing experience of God, being continually nourished and nurtured by the Lord's presence, has the power to shape one's life. Where many believers fail is in the surrendered response to God's gracious movement towards us. With unapologetic biblical and theological integrity and grounding, Dr. Walter offers faithful perspective on worship that has been conditioned not only by his extensive leadership experience and academic preparation, but more deeply out of the depths of his heart of worship. He is a worshipper. Beyond the typical expressions of contemporary praise and classical liturgy, he understands the holistic nature of our living, which is meant to be worship.

Very insightful is Dr. Walter's encouragement for people of faith to embrace that which cannot be predicted, explained or managed. Warfare, transition, crisis, darkness, disappointment and pain all become powerful tools in the hands of God that has the potential to move us to worship as no other means could. Here again many believers forfeit the opportunity for worship in spirit and in truth as they resist the more challenging facets of our living that require the relinquishment of all need for comfort or control.

Unlike many written spiritual resources in circulation today that remain in the abstract and are disconnected from the lives of real people, Dr. Walter is a thoughtful practitioner and gives the reader tools to be able to navigate the way forward into a richer experience of God with stories, anecdotes and personal reflections. Grounded in the covenant promises of God to those who believe, he leads the reader through the multiple approaches to worship.

Dr. Walter strikes at the heart of where authentic worship ultimately leads: *Transformation*! Lives are touched and changed when one is encountered by the living God. People are not "sinners in the hands of an angry God" as British theologian Jonathan Edwards preached long ago, but rather, worshippers in the heart of a loving God. With Jesus as the perfect Example and Redeemer, the Father invites us to worship and be made whole.

Dr. Glenn Walter courageously opens a portal to an experience that all humans have shared or will share at some point – grief and loss – the lot of humankind. In a vulnerable and loving way, the reader is walked through deeply personal losses and the transformation that can ensue. In *Transformational Worship*, Dr. Walter seeks to show that authentic worship changes lives. It heals wounds and opens the heart to hear the God who so often speaks in *a still small voice.*

~ ***Rev. Dr. C. Lynn Nakamura***
Professor Emerita
Trinity Lutheran Seminary, Columbus, Ohio

Chapter 1

WORSHIPPING THROUGH THE UNEXPLAINABLE

A Mother's *Unexplainable* Love

Learning how to worship through challenging situations is often a painstaking process. As Christians, we are not immune to unforeseen crises, tragedies, or unthinkable acts of devastation. God's mercy is extended to both the wicked and righteous. The Heavenly Father sends rain on the just and the unjust alike (Matthew 5:44). It is imperative that we learn how to worship God whether on mountain or in the valley.

The Christian narrative does not leave room for timidity and doubt. Either you believe the record of events concerning the life of Jesus Christ or you do not. The Bible is replete with examples of people demonstrating faith in our Lord and Savior during challenging times. Should we who are blessed to be alive in post modernity be any different? I think not!

One of the most difficult times of my life was enduring my mother's illnesses and subsequent death. The opening of Charles Dickens' novel, "A Tale of Two Cities" best summarizes this period of my life:

"It was the best of times, it was the worst of times, it was the age of wisdom, it was the age of foolishness…"

I seriously lack the speech mechanisms, adjectives and literary expressions to either adequately or accurately write about my love for mom. Diane Marie Walter was the *quintessential* lady. She was many things to many people. She was poet, philosopher, cultured debutante, community organizer, local beautician, family chef and oh yes, family disciplinarian.

My mom and I shared many sacred moments. We were especially close. One moment particularly summarized our inextricably connected lives. She and I attended Mt. Calvary's New Year's watch-night service. It was a very evangelical service. Afterwards, we waited for our transportation, yet, he never arrived. Therefore, we decided to walk home. Thank goodness it wasn't very cold, and we lived less than one mile from the church. As we slowly walked down Oakhill Avenue, it began to gently snow. The snowfall was calm, tranquil and quite beautiful. Effortlessly she articulated thanksgiving for living long enough to see me graduate from high school. In retrospect, I have often wondered if mom wasn't endeavoring to tell me something that perhaps I wasn't ready to receive. My mom was young and beautiful. She was only 32 years old. Amazingly, no sounds of loud gunfire rang in the air. We began reminiscing about the goodness of God down through the years.

There was a contentment emanating from mom that night. She was in perfect spiritual harmony. She spoke about life in metaphorical terms. Intently, I listened to her wisdom and expressions of gratitude. Throughout our dialogue, mom conveyed love for each of her children.

Worshipping *Through* Mother's Challenge

During the following years, Diane's health began to slowly diminish. She was diagnosed with narcolepsy. Narcolepsy is a condition characterized by an extreme tendency to fall asleep. This illness was particularly troublesome. It interfered with mom's independence and ability to drive. Next, diabetes became an issue for the lovely former lead majorette. My mom was required to take insulin shots before age 36. Narcolepsy, diabetes, followed by psoriasis was more than she could manage. Mom began losing her thick black Cherokee shoulder-length hair. Her weight gain was significant. The loss of good health at a very young age was unbearable. Worriment and unhealthy dietary habits became a toxic daily routine.

By the age of 40, doctors, medical treatments and prescriptions were very much a part of mom's monthly routine. I remember wondering, why so much pain? Why must my mother endure this irrational suffering? My great-grandmother, the mother of Beulah Temple Holiness Church, never suffered like this.

My grandmother had some challenges in her later years but nothing comparable to what mom was experiencing. It is difficult to rationalize human suffering. It is especially difficult to rationalize the suffering of your loved one.

Making matters worse, if that were possible, entered church folks. Like Hollywood characters from a casting agency they came with religious platitudes and canned church homilies. "God won't put more on you than you can bear." "The Lord knows what He's doing, Diane!" And of course, my favorite, "The Lord gon' bring you out of this, Di!" Like Job's friends, these people invaded mom's personal space with nonsensical religious rhetoric on a weekly routine. Who were these people? Where on earth did they get these nonbiblical notions? God was not punishing my mom with diabetes. God was not a charter member of Gangstaz R Us. He did not summon Guido the Assassin, to infect my mom with an incurable disease. Diabetes is a result of the pancreas' inability to sufficiently produce insulin.

I offer sincere transparency here, my attitude toward church folks categorically began to change during mom's physical weakening. What I witnessed during mom's health crisis was not Christ-like. It was "Churchanity!" Yes, it sounded like Christianity but it did not possess the integrity, authenticity and loving-kindness of Christlikeness. Churchanity is a form of Christianity but it lacks genuine commitment, sincerity and conviction. It is mostly comprised of local church culture, religious rules and denominational traditions that make the Word of God to no effect (Mark 7:13).

Worshipping *Through* the Battle

What happened next can only be described as a blur of consultations, assessments, treatments, procedures and what seemed like innumerable hospitalizations in multiple medical centers. I was traveling to Youngstown, Ohio on a weekly basis although working on an associate degree in another city hundreds of miles away. I developed a worshipful routine that consisted of meeting with the medical team, analyzing information and heading straight to the throne of God in prayer. Eventually, I learned how to transform the atmosphere of a hospital room into a conduit that welcomed the presence of Jehovah God.

My mom was lying in South Side Hospital the day I graduated from military college with my two-year degree. I graduated at the top of my class, but it seemed anticlimactic. Diane Marie wasn't there to celebrate it with me. Academically, the next two years were the best of times; both mom and dad managed to make it to the bachelor's degree ceremony. They watched their son graduate magna cum laude.

It was the worst of times because mother's health was steadily deteriorating. Over the next few years, hospital admissions became the norm. In addition to the monthly hospital visits, dialysis became a weekly event. Unlike many others, mom never suspected God was chastising her. She remained steadfast. Her testimonial became a source of strength for me.

First, the family was informed that if her toes were removed on her right foot the infection would be averted. However, the infection did not cease. Next, her foot was removed. The enormity of reality was too overwhelming for my father. He asked me to serve as the family liaison for all medical decisions. When the infection ceased from spreading, I decided that it was better to have her entire leg removed at one time. It was one of the most painstaking decisions that I have ever made.

Unfortunately, my mother's surgical intervention was incorrectly performed. Her wounds were closed utilizing metal staples. Metal staples should not have been used on a diabetic patient. Exacerbating the already difficult situation, my sister informed me that the medical transport team accidentally dropped our mother while transporting her to dialysis.

As I traveled back to Youngstown, I was so enraged that I literally wanted to physically inflict as much pain as possible into all irresponsible parties but especially the inept transport team. God, however, had another plan. After arriving at Saint Elizabeth Medical Center, I was contacted by Dr. Earnest Perry. He was not only a brilliant and noted surgeon. He was also a Christian. In addition to being a Christian physician, Dr. Perry was the Chairman of the Department of Surgery at Forum Health – Western Reserve Care System. He was also an Associate Professor of Clinical Surgery at the Northeastern Ohio Universities College of Medical and Pharmacy. In other words, God sent this abundantly qualified man to help my family.

He met me in my mother's room. To date, I don't know how he found me. He told me, "Glenn, I'm going to take care of your mother!" He explained specifically what he was going to do. He reassured me that his medical team would do everything within their power to ensure my mother would not suffer unnecessarily.

As soon as Dr. Perry, God's medical servant leader, departed mom's room; I began uncontrollably crying. Tears were streaming. I wanted to be angry. I wanted to punish the people who hurt Diane. But my anger was replaced with unexplainable worship. My will was, once again broken. This entire episode transpired during Thanksgiving weekend.

While sitting in the apartment contemplating my recently diagnosed intestinal infection, unemployment status and overall mental health, it occurred to me that I needed God more now than ever before. Diane's predicament was always in the forefront of my mind. I spoke to my sister often over the next thirty days. She and I collaborated on every detail appertaining to our parents. Not only were we concerned about mom, our father's mental condition became of interest to us as well.

During this period of my life, I learned to stop looking for conclusive answers in so many presentations. I learned that my personal connection with God was far more vital than listening to sermons, choirs, testimonials or reading spiritual commentaries. There is no substitute for a personal relationship with God through the intercessory power of the Holy Spirit! Sermons can encourage. Testimonials can help you overcome. Spiritual reading materials have the potential to inspire. Nothing, and I mean absolutely nothing, can take the place of personal intercession! You must cultivate and develop an in-depth meaningful relationship with God.

Every day became a new worshipful experience. Every day I had to learn to shut my eyes and walk by faith. The realities of my sensory perception became my spiritual enemy. I learned the true meaning of faith. I learned that faith was the substance of my future. Faith became the building matter for my very existence. Faith was the necessary ingredient that provided hope. I learned to worship without musical instrumentation, reading Bibles or singing hymns. Most importantly, I learned to worship without sitting on a church pew or participating in a church service. Worship became an integral part of my daily routine. Worship became a transformative experience. In fact, it is impossible to genuinely worship God and not undergo a transformation. This unimaginable situation was teaching me how to worship through the unexplainable.

On December 30th, my phone rang, it was my sister Michelle. She informed me that another infection was detected in mom's left leg. In addition to the infection, mom was beginning to lose her eyesight. The following day, on New Year's Eve, I traveled back to Youngstown with heaviness of heart. After arriving at Saint Elizabeth's Medical Center, I met with the lead physician. He informed me that a second amputation was necessary to prevent the spread of gangrene. I was willing to consent to the intervention with the stipulation that Dr. Ernest Perry performed the surgery. He consented. I spent New Year's Day in the hospital with my mother, a double amputee.

The surgery was successful. My mother was approved to come home about a week after the surgery. Caring for my mother became overwhelming for my father. My sister, a licensed LPN voluntarily agreed to become the primary caregiver for my mother. Chelly and her husband, Dessie, lovingly moved my mom into their spacious home.

Endeavoring to explain the dynamism of caring for your mother because your father is either unwilling or emotionally unable is rather complicated. This period of our lives was beleaguered with multi-generational, intrafamilial differences. My dad, Tom, clearly understood the chief requirement for giving upward mobility to any family was sustained employment. However, he struggled with the concept of emotionality and its fundamental relevance in family structure. My father possessed a work ethic like the Old Testament patriarch, Boaz. Dad was elegant in dress and style. He wore silk suits and drove a Cadillac Coup Deville. However, Tom Walter, could never be accused of being overly communicative. He was not a socially cultured type of guy. Dad's idea of Shakespeare was literally shaking a spear at us for whatever perturbed him on any given day. Mom drove a Buick LeSabre and it was usually filled with groceries or children, sometimes both. She was the designated matriarchal nurturer. And now, operating in place of our family caregiver was the nurturing heiress, my sister, Chelly.

Worshipping *Through* Transition

My sister did an outstanding job caring for our mother. She meticulously attended to mom's every need. Although, Chelly and Dessie had three children of their own, I never heard one complaint about the difficulties involved with being a caretaker for mom. On many occasions, mom and I would spend hours talking in her bedroom. Her complete loss of vision in no way diminished her mental acuity. Our philosophical discussions were as robust and meaningful as ever. Discerning the meaning of Plato's cave was one of our favorite debates. I discerned however, that mom's sphere of focus was intensely more Christ-centric. Her interest in Plato's Republic and Sigmund Freud's interpretations waned considerably. Diane Marie was preparing for her transition into eternity. I was, however not ready to accept the obviousness of the truth: nothing can outlive its appointed season.

It was early in the morning when the phone rang. I don't remember the specific time. I do, however, remember Chelly exclaiming, "Glenn, we have to take mom back to the hospital." In retrospect, it was something very different about this voyage back to Youngstown. Innumerable times I made that journey. However, there was something distinctly different this time. It was a very mentally arduous drive. I wrestled in my spirit. Like the Old Testament patriarch Jacob, I insisted on not accepting Jehovah's sovereignty. I was not ready to let her go. I was not ready to bid the queen farewell.

Upon arriving at Saint Elizabeth Medical Center on what seemed like the one hundredth visit, I ascertained the room number and entered Diane's room very circumspectly. There was solemnness in the atmosphere. She seemed to be in great spirits. I asked mom how she was feeling. I will never forget her positive response, "the Lord is good." The next two weeks can only be described as spiritual. I refused to leave her side. I literally stayed in the hospital for two weeks. On one occasion mom began to have chest pains. She went into cardiac arrest. I remember hearing the words, code blue!

What happened next could only be described as a blur. I vaguely recalled hearing, "Mr. Walter, we are honoring your wishes, no defibrillation treatment will be administered." In lieu of electronic shocks or CPR, mom was given an injection of adrenaline. It revived her.

I didn't quote any Bible verses. I offered no deep meaningful stratospheric prayers. I said absolutely nothing. I sat slumped on a window ledge with my hands clasped together with tears rolling off my face. There was, however, one name that I repeatedly whispered. It is a highly exalted name. That name was Jesus. Every fear, doubt, concern and vexing distress was released each time I articulated the phonetic sound composing the name, Jesus.

Although my momentary choice was silence, I was entirely cognizant of the emergency procedure to restart mom's heart. Interestingly, adrenaline restart is no longer used. However, it revived her. Upon exiting the room, I was notified that my father was being transported to St. E's emergency room. Not possible, I thought! The dream-like moment became a nightmare! Calmly, I walked away from the cardiac care unit and entered the emergency room. There, in an isolated room, dad lay quietly still. He seemed unaffected by the weightiness of his situation. The atmosphere seemed somewhat sullen. I asked, "Dad are you able to describe your pain?" "Yes," he replied. He began to explain his discomfort. Afterwards, he reassured me that he was going to be just fine. Tom expressed his concerns for mom. He was apologetic for his lack of involvement in mom's health crisis.

I excused myself and stepped out of the room for a moment. As I stood outside of the room I begin calling on the name of the Lord. Over the years, calling on the name of the Lord while experiencing something unexplainably painful, has become a spiritual "panic room." The Bible exclaims, "The name of the Lord is a strong tower: the righteous runneth into it, and is safe" (Proverbs 18:10).

There are going to be times in this life when crisis seemingly becomes the norm. During those times, panic is often not an option.

Worship is a means whereby one releases fear, trepidation, apprehension and insecurity into the hands of an omniscient, omnipresence and omnipotent God that is incapable of failing!

I sensed the very presence of God during that moment. His presence was reassuring. It spoke volumes to my human instability. The awesomeness of His power reassured me that the same God who watches over patients in the cardiac care unit also simultaneously sustains the lives of those in the emergency room. His presence reassured me that there is nothing transpiring on the face of the earth that escapes His awareness! I exited the room of worship and entered the closet of prayer.

I began to pray and ask God for strength to be whatever my family needed for this hour. They needed someone strong; I was weak. They needed someone calm; I was nervous. They needed a faithful stalwart that emoted confidence in God. I was not that person. But through the power of prayer God transformed me to be that person. As I concluded my prayer, my father arose from the emergency room bed and said to me, "Son, I will be fine. You need to go back and stay with Diane."

The next week changed my life forever. I spent a great deal of time communicating with my mother about faith, love, and life. Each day it was a new worshipful experience. I had the opportunity to embrace her character and godliness as a steadfast worshiper.

I never heard my mother complain about her predicament. The last week of my mother's life was emotionally challenging. On one occasion, I distinctly remember standing by the elevators while staring out the window. Although spiritually encouraged, I was emotionally and physically exhausted. As the elevator bell chimed and the door slowly opened, a very familiar person exited. It was my brother in Christ, Elder Eric Colter. This brother drove four hours one-way just to sit with me and be a blessing to my soul! He greeted my mother in Jesus's name. He asked her, "Mother, how are you doing today?" She replied, "The Lord is good!"

Pastor Colter remained there at the hospital with me for the remainder of the day. This brother agreed to take my wife and children home. The trip took an additional two hours out of his way; nevertheless, this excellent man of God stood by our side during the time of crisis.

The next day my mother was moved to a different floor. She was placed in observation. I was extraordinarily grateful that she was disconnected from all monitors. She was no longer required to have intravenous needles. We prayed together as we waited for her lunch to arrive. She was in excellent spirits. And then, with a prophetical voice, this profound declaration was made, "Glenn, I have gone as far as I can go with you. Now, son, you must run on for yourself."

Like the disciples, who often did not understand the meaning of Jesus' parables; I did not comprehend the moment prior to her transition. Immediately, after she said these words, the dietitian entered the room with her lunch. As so many times before, I identified the food groups and their locations as if her plate was the face of a clock. That is, the potatoes are at 12 o'clock, the green beans are at 3 o'clock, and the turkey is at 9 o'clock on the plate. Of course, mom insisted that her fruit cocktail be in a separate container positioned at 9 o'clock. Her independence was paramount even until the end. I kissed her. I expressed my love to her for the final time. We worshiped God together for the last time in this dimension. I informed her that I was returning to Columbus to submit resumes to potential employers. Before exiting the room, mom blessed me. As I climbed into the van, it was a feeling of ill at ease. The car phone rang after traveling approximately ten miles from the hospital. My wife said, "Glenn, go back to the hospital. It's urgent." A plethora of thoughts rushed through the corridors of my mind while jetting back.

The elevator doors opened. My heart was pounding. I scurried toward mom's room. The countenances of the nursing staff informed me that haste was no longer necessary. They refused to make eye contact with me. That's when I knew, mom had transitioned. I slowly entered her room.

The Holy Spirit brought two scriptures to the forefront of my mind: "Behold, what manner of love the Father hath bestowed upon us, that we should be called the Sons of God: therefore the world knoweth us not, because it knew him not. Beloved, now are we the Sons of God, and it doth not yet appear what we shall be: but we know that, when he shall appear, we shall be like him; for we shall see him as he is" (1 John 3: 1-2).

It is difficult to explain surreality. It is an intensifying feeling of irrational unbelievability. Surreality, however, is the best word to accurately describe that moment. Diane would never suffer again. She was completely absolved from all pain associated with this earthly realm. Finally, my mother was resting in the presence of the Almighty God. I grappled with conflicting emotions. For a moment, I felt abandonment. While feeling abandonment, simultaneously, a sense of reassurance rested in my spirit. And although I felt grief, there was a blessed reassurance that God had prepared me to deal with this moment and the forthcoming future. It occurred to me that Diane prophetically spoke of this moment. She tried to inform me of this very moment when she stated, "I've gone as far with you as I can, now you must run on for yourself." Yes, the baton that was placed securely in her hands had been transferred to me. Now, it was my turn to run the leg of a spiritual race. It was my privilege to serve the next generation with the transformative message of good news concerning the death, burial and resurrection of Jesus Christ, our Lord and Savior.

Through this experience, Mom taught me how to worship through the unexplainable. Diane's tenacious sagacity set a standard for me to adhere. Your spiritual conviction must be resolute and unflinching. Our lives are truly an open book. The pages of that book must resoundingly declare that for me to live is Christ and to die is gain (Philippians 1:21). She didn't foolishly accuse God of punishing her. Diane Marie maintained her integrity. My mother chose to worship instead of complaining about maltreatment, neglect, isolation or sickness. I learned that worship is a choice! The distinguished lady who gave birth to me fought a good fight. Yes, she finished her race. Mom kept the faith. And now, a crown of righteousness, which the Lord, the righteous judge will give her on the day of His return. After exiting the room, my mind began reflecting. The previous ten months were emotionally wrenching. I wondered why Raymond, my mother's brother never called and visited only once. This man brought a worthless stuffed rabbit to a blind double amputee. I questioned why Mary, my mother's sister, neglected to call and visited only once. She and Raymond came to the hospital on the same day. And most glaringly, I pondered why my mother's pastor never called or visited. Was he too busy? Why didn't he send one of the clergy? The congregational size was less than one hundred members.

Surely someone must have noticed her absence. There were no calls, home visits or cards from anyone associated with that ministry. She had been repeatedly hospitalized for more than eighteen months. Where were all those church people? Where were all the prayer warriors, missionaries and deacons? Where were those stellar ministers who loved standing in front of the congregation with their clergy collars, designer suits and Thompson Chain Bibles? The only clergy that visited were from my Mt. Calvary Pentecostal Church. Those ministers were faithful men of God. And besides the negligent church folks, our own extended family members were missing in action as well. How many children did my mother help raise? In my opinion, too many! Mom changed numerous dirty diapers of children that did not live in her house. Diane Marie fed and clothed children and teenagers claiming to be family members from every part of Youngstown. Sometimes, we, the original Walter children would wake up to what appeared to be a community breakfast for Black Americans! But I didn't recognize these Black folks? They were not members of the Walter family. They didn't look like my brother Tony or sister Chelly. They looked like a mixture of Black leprechauns, hillbillies and lumberjacks at the Last Supper! Not one of these ungrateful African descendants came to see my mom during her illness. And that includes one famous NFL nephew who travels the country telling everyone about my mother's testimony. He also failed to visit the hospital although Diane helped raise him, too.

Now, dad's words rang in my spirit like the horn on a semi-truck: "Son, if you find two friends in this life, you've done well!"

The only consistent non-family member who visited mom regularly was Ms. Katherine. We affectionately referred to her as Ms. Kay. She was not a member of mom's church. And, as God would have it, she was an employee of St. E's dietitian staff. Ms. Kay made sure that every member of our family ate whenever we were visiting mom. She was a consistent friend to my mother throughout the years. I don't ever recall her bringing imported olive oil to pray for my mother. I do, however, remember her bringing groceries to my mother and father's house. I distinctly remember her leaving money on the table for whatever was needed. She didn't wear a clergy collar. She didn't verbalize any ecumenical prayers.

She never requested any recognition. She came quietly and departed the same way. Ms. Kay had a beautiful spirit. She avoided fan-fare and grandstanding. It wasn't necessary. Nope, she just befriended and loved Diane Marie. How about that?

A collage of abstract questions continued to race through the corridors of my mind while standing outside of that hospital room. My thought processes were interrupted as the funeral home staff arrived. I could not bear to see my mother escorted out of the room in a body bag on a gurney.

As I begin slowly walking down that familiar hallway, the image of that morphine drip somehow reappeared. I must have watched that morphine drip for hours at a time. I'm not exactly sure why this image reappeared. Perhaps it spoke to the state of my mental condition.

During the next couple of days, we began preparing for mom's homegoing service. I spent those days sitting at Chelly's dining room table staring into nothingness. I watched the sunrise and set from the same room. After hours of staring, finally, I was able to write mom's obituary. The next day Tony, Chelly and I collaborated on the program for mom's homegoing service. Chelly selected all clothing items for mom's viewing. This was one of the most grievous affairs of my entire life. I must have experienced the entire spectrum of emotions in a matter of hours. My emotions vacillated from happiness to anger in a matter of minutes.

The day before the homegoing services, an unusual calmness encapsulated me. I could literally feel the presence of God resting on me. I was completely serene. I was able to speak words of reassurance to my dad. He was still in shock. Dad could barely function. I was supernaturally able to greet all extended family members, peaceably, including my mother's brother and sister.

Worshipping *Through* the Unspeakable

Finally, the nightfall came. It was necessary for me to be alone. While calmly sitting on Chelly's sofa, it was time for me to have a conversation with the Lord. He and I had some unfinished business to discuss. I wanted to know why did my mother have to suffer? I wanted to know why evil people prospered while righteous people suffered? There was no need to conceal my feelings. God already knew what was in my heart. My thoughts and feelings were completely transparent to Him. After voicing my displeasure to the Almighty, sudden weariness came over me and immediately I fell asleep.

The Holy Ghost ministered to me. I AM the God who is above you (Psalms 95:3). I AM He that undergirds you (Deuteronomy 33:27). I AM the Spirit surrounding you (Psalms 5:12). I AM the God who dwells in you (1 John 4:13-15) and through you (Galatians 2:20). Supernaturally, the Lord imparted strength to me. He provided revelatory knowledge about my mother's condition. God's presence was exceedingly apparent as I arose the next day. There was an unusual anointing resting in my spirit. For years the expression "God's anointed vessel" was non-evidentiary to me. It was a church cultural phrase not necessarily applicable to anything in our post-modern world. Before getting up, the Word of the Lord was given to me for the homegoing service.

Suddenly, the awesomeness of anointing became obvious as I walked through the living room worshipping. The Spirit of the Lord was upon me. He was anointing me for today's assignment. The burden was too great for me to face without His favor. My sorrowful heaviness and human anguish subsided in His presence.

The moment was engulfing. I stood somewhere between heaven and earth. I endeavored to comfort Tom, Anthony and Michelle. Dad's disbelief left him somewhat emotionally paralyzed. Although that was to be expected his health gave occasion for concern. I reassured cousins, nephews, nieces, grandchildren and everyone else. Slowly, the L.E. Black Funeral cars stopped in front of Chelly's house. Amid dealing with death, a senseless discussion ensued. My aunt decided that she should ride in the family car. I quietly asked, "Dad what do you want?" "Son handle it, please." "Auntie, you are not riding with us. Find another car." She looked at my expression, "Ok, nephew," was her kind response. Our ride to the Chapel was intense.

To date, my recollection of entering that room is nonexistent. Once inside, I couldn't stand to look at Mom. So, instead of standing awkwardly behind the bier, I decided to extend appreciation to Diane's guests for showing support. While shaking hands mom's pastor approached me.

"Glenn, I am so sorry for your lost," he said. "Your mother was a wonderful Saint of God. I'd like to extend my condolences to the entire family. May I say a few words this afternoon?" This man was either shamelessly arrogant (incorrigible) or simply dull of reasoning (obtuse). I felt a carnal impulse to just break buck wild on this Negro! Jesus! Help me Lord, please! That was my silent prayer. I said, "As her pastor, you never visited or called my mother. Now, you're not going to say anything at this homegoing service!" What I really wanted to do was not very Christ-like. Mom would have disapproved. Thank God, my brother didn't see him. There would have been another funeral!

Finally, it was time to honor Diane Marie. Hundreds respectfully gathered to pay homage to a royal and stately queen. The homegoing service accurately conveyed her life and legacy. After proper musical tributes and poetic renditions, I was poised to eulogize the woman who gave birth to me. The sermon was entitled, "Bon Voyage." Afterwards, we gathered for the interment. Leaving the gravesite was more difficult than the actual homegoing service. During our ride to the traditional church dinner, a second sermon was graciously provided to mom's brother and sister. The sermonic focus was on sibling dereliction and shameful neglect. Why not? I had a captured audience.

The family and guests arrived at Ms. Kay's church after the interment. Kay kept blessing us even after mom was gone.

I did my best to be hospitable. There are many Black church traditions that I do not understand although I have spent most of my life submerged in church culture. Entertaining people immediately after burying your loved one is a very straining tradition. My father was not enjoying himself. Neither my brother nor my sister was particularly ingratiating at the dinner. Of course, in the Black church, a meal after interments are properly called respites (a short period of time when you can stop doing something difficult or unpleasant). Mom was especially gifted at interacting with people during social events. Unfortunately, her husband and children were not.

After dinner, our family was emotionally and physically exhausted. Everyone was quiet during the ride back to Chelly's house. Tom sorely needed to be alone. He immediately returned home. Chelly and Tony absolutely refused to interact with our extended family. They departed together. I was left alone with my sordid cousins. Once again, the original Walter children would be invaded by a community of ungrateful Negros that didn't look like us. As I said previously, not one of these ruffians called or came to see my mom during her illness. Now, they were at mom's funeral. A Samson anointing came over me. I intended to rid my sister's house of the Philistines with a donkey's jawbone, if necessary! Repeatedly, I heard my mother's soprano voice saying, "Glenn Thomas, please be nice."

Thankfully, they did not stay for an extended period. Tony and Chelly eventually returned. I missed them badly.

This was our time. We laughed. We talked. We cried. We were closer now than ever before. Finally, Diane's three children were sitting up straight at the dinner table behaving like "civilized" people. Mom would have been proud of her gifted prodigies. We had learned how to worship through the unexplainable.

A Love Song For Chelly

Love *at* Birth

Michelle Lynn was angelic! She was my childhood joy. Various names were discussed prior to her birth. The need to select a name for my newborn sister "charade" seemingly continued forever. Finally, mom asked, "Glenn, what do you think we should call her?" I answered definitely, "She should be called, Michelle!" Mom quipped, "Why Michelle?" "Well, Michelle is the prettiest girl in my class." Mom smiled. "Oh, really, do you like Michelle?" Diane Marie just couldn't let it go. It was her inquisitive Socratic nature. Her right to know superseded my right to privacy. "No, mom, she's just the cutest girl in the class." Of course, Mom knew better but she acquiesced to my evasiveness. After a few moments of silence, Mom agreed that the name Michelle was regal enough for her newborn child providing it was a girl. When Michelle Lynn finally arrived home her beauty was indescribable!

Without comparison, she was the most beautiful baby I had ever seen. By the age of three, everyone, especially my grandfather was under the influence of Chelly. On one occasion, Grandpa Louis, decided to make his famous ice cream utilizing snow as his key ingredient. Finally, he invited the entire family to the kitchen after what seemed like hours of preparation. Everyone quickly gathered except for mom and Chelly.

They were the last to enter the kitchen. Mom stood at the bottom of the stairwell; while princess Chelly made a grand entrance. Michelle Lynn was wearing a white lace dress, white lace gloves, white lace socks and white shoes. As she walked toward the kitchen table her shoulder–length long black banana curls bounced in unison. Grandpa had an epic meltdown! He took five dollars out of his wallet and gave it to his most *favorite* granddaughter! This act of benevolence was equivalent to the Grinch receiving salvation on Christmas Day! I have never seen this man give anyone more than a dollar, ever! The most money grandpa ever gave me was thirty–five cents. And when I get to heaven, he'll probably ask for it back, plus interest.

My sister had a gracious personality and a hospitable spirit. Her attitude exuded compassion. Of course, my attitude radiated with combat readiness. I displayed all the hospitality of an African Zulu warrior. Michelle Lynn was wired differently. Throughout her teenage years she remained introverted and yet, remarkably inquisitive.

My Friend, My Sister

There was never a better friend than my sister. There was never a better sister than Michelle Lynn.

Her loving compassion was without comparison. Her unselfishness enabled her to care for the sick, defend the weak, feed the hungry & nurture the abandon.

We were true lovers of books, in essence, twin bibliophiles. We were inextricably connected. Perhaps it was the countless days spent together in the South Side Public Library. Maybe innumerable outings, coupled with endless dialog, helped solidify our sibling bond. Or, possibly an uncommon brother and sister connection was forged during the elementary school years. Whenever my parents – mom who worked at Kessler Products and dad who worked at GM – departed early for work; Glenn was responsible for ensuring that Anthony and Michelle were properly prepared for school.

Although, there isn't one specific measurable event or act that bonded us together, one thing is certain, as siblings, we shared a pheromonal twin-like connection. As we grew older, our inter-connectedness increased. My spirit discerned Chelly's emotional challenges without her verbally disclosing them. Youngstown, Ohio was often listed on the FBI's most dangerous cities in America. Many young urbanites chose a life of corruption and criminality. Unlike many of her peers, Chelly opted for a career in medical care. Her preference was to care for the sick. As a licensed practicing nurse (LPN), providing service to others became a way of life. Understandably, our mother's health challenges played a major role in her career choice. She made me ridiculously proud! During our many telephone conversations, she expressed a determination to excel in life.

Soon, a young husband and three children became the center of her universe. The little princess with banana curls who accompanied me to community events and PG movies was a grown woman. It happened so quickly. In retrospect, it felt as though her life was played fast-forward. The radiant darling with a picture-perfect smile who held my hand as we walk down Breaden Street; was now a wife and a mother of three: Tierra, Dessie and Denzel. By societal standards Chelly was successful. However, there was an absence of contentment in her eyes. I did not discern personal or professional satisfaction. Inwardly, there was something missing. There was a spiritual longing and an absence of contentment.

On several occasions she would travel alone to my home. Those times were precious to me. We would discuss our fondest childhood memories. Those memories were filled with mom's parental homilies and Freudian antidotes. But our most heartfelt fondest memories were based on mom's lessons about our Lord and Savior, Jesus Christ. We spent innumerable hours listening to substantive sermons by various preachers. Afterwards, we would discuss the sermon. Preaching and teaching is meaningless unless the content is relevant to the listeners. Michelle was desirous to have a more meaningful relationship with God. Her loyalties were, well, somewhat divided while endeavoring to follow the Word of God and keep peace in her home.

Therefore, sermonic content about boats, planes, automobiles and mansions were irrelevant and quite frankly, worthless. Although young, beautiful and professionally accomplished; a spiritual healing for her fatigued soul was needed. This healing could come only through the power and purity of Christ's Word!

Chelly was a burgeoning 24-year-old wife and mother with a promising future. What should have been her field of dreams seemed like a nightmare on Elm Street. My sister carried her burdens deep inside. Despite her marital challenges, she took on the responsibilities of being the primary caretaker for our mother. Diane would go home to be with the Lord within a year of living with Chelly. This loss was catastrophic to everyone, but it was especially hard on Michelle.

Ready, *Set*, Transformed

A profound spiritual determination grew within my sister during the next two years. Michelle decided to move away from the medical profession. Although she never disclosed her reasoning to me, it was apparently obvious. A professional environmental change was needed. Not only did she make professional changes, I noticed socio-economic changes being made as well. Something spiritually was happening. The permeating weariness was rapidly diminishing. Old acquaintances were being excommunicated. People filled with negativity and toxicity was hurriedly replaced by those with wholesome perspectives. Watching Michelle Lynn rid her life of bad characters was equivalent to watching an Olympic ice skater flawlessly twirling like a tornado at the end of a perfect routine. She was on a spiritual speed cycle. As her brother, I felt like running the aisles and speaking in unknown tongues. The elimination of Ouija Slim, Phat Jim, Kool Moe Lem, and Spicy Hot Kim was perfectly fine by me, good riddance! It took some time, but purging was necessary. The distractions had to be eliminated.

A few months later during a leisurely Sunday afternoon my phone rang. It was my favorite sister, of course. Her voice was beaming with joy. "Glenn, guess what happened to me today during church," she asked. "What?" I anxiously inquired. She confidently responded, "I received the Holy Spirit!"

The best two words to describe that moment are stupendous gratification.

For years, we discussed the emptiness of endeavoring to find fulfillment through knowledge about Christ. Having knowledge of Christ is not equivalent to having relationship with Christ. Yes, it is true that one must possess knowledge of Christ before submitting to him. But no man can come to Jesus Christ unless he is drawn to him (St. John 6:44). That day the Lord knocked on Michelle's heart and she opened the door and invited Him in. She confessed with her mouth and believed in her heart. She was not only baptized in water but with spiritual fire.

Dessie and Michelle sold their house not long after mom's transition. The painful memories were too much. Finding the new place was no easy task. But the many weeks of searching finally paid off. It was my desire to celebrate this milestone with my sister's family. There was an unusual excitement in my spirit while traveling to Youngstown. I longed to see their newly built residence. Upon arrival, I took my family to a relative. Our children needed to relax and unwind. An enormous sense of satisfaction came over me as I approached their newly built condominium. It was glistening white. The complex was resplendently charming and very befitting of her personality.

I slowly pulled into the driveway. I wanted to relish the moment. When she opened the door, I grabbed her! I was so very proud of my sister.

In that moment my mind started wondering. What would mom think? What would mom say to her baby daughter now?

As we embraced, tears flowed from our eyes. It is one of the most memorable moments of my life. I languished in the moment. This was an older brother's spiritual self-actualization. I never wanted to disappoint Michelle. She constantly looked up to me. At two years old, her smile was an incentive to excel. I helped to change diapers, warmed bottles and put her to sleep. I was there when she took her first steps in those white Stride-Rite Baby Walking Shoes. I was there when at three years old; she climbed on her green Hasbro Inchworm. Mother and I applauded baby girl's gallant effort for peddling the Western Flyer tricycle for the first time.

Chelly was our princess. It was not a sacrifice for Anthony to ensure her safe arrival at school. And, if anyone harassed her, we would pulverize them. As she grew older, my brother and I beat the living daylights out of at least of half dozen lame brothers who tried to date Chelly. After all, we thought most guys in Youngstown were probable suspects in criminal activities. Anyone attempting to approach our sister had to undergo Glenn's and Anthony's assessment. Of course, there were none worthy! So, we beat them. These were not your average physical struggles.

These public spectacles were equivalent to WWE tag team beat downs. Most of Chelly's suitors never returned to 135 Breaden Street. I once heard my brother tell a young man, "If I ever see you come near my sister, I'll shoot you!" I never saw him again, ever.

Chelly experienced her first official date at around 15 years old. I remember that day very well. I was home visiting. A handsome young man pulled a shiny car into our parent's driveway. Instead of getting out of the car and coming into the house like a respectable gentleman, this rascal blew the horn. Big mistake. I bolted out the front door and began re-educating him. As I physically ministered to him, mom came outside and yelled, "Glenn Thomas, leave that boy alone! Mom asked him, "Young man, are you alright?" Tony was about to tag into the ring. Diane, however, escorted him past Tony. Wearing a frown, she said, "Michelle will never have anybody if it's left up to you and Tony." She continued, "Both of you need to go somewhere and sit down. Act civilized!" Being civilized was not our Modus Operandi. We preferred tag team punishment! Mom, of course, had other plans for her daughter.

The condominium was breathtaking! It was incredibly spacious. Packing boxes lined the walls. Yes, Diane Marie would have loved it. Dessie was at work and the children were at Grandma's house. She and I unpacked boxes for hours.

We hadn't talked like this for months. We reminisced about our lives and familial experiences. We took a break and ate.

During lunch she shared her renewed perspective for Christ. She recalled the vivid details associated with the infilling of the Holy Spirit. Never did Michelle speak with such abundant boldness. Her teeming attitude was that of a new convert! The rich and pure abundant confidence in God was refreshing! It sounded evangelistic. The spring of Living Water was overflowing. She was beaming inexhaustibly. I loved it and insisted on hearing more!

The evening time was rapidly approaching. I started hanging up the pictures. I could tell we were making progress. Cabinets were being filled. Dresser drawers were being lined neatly with children's clothing. While unpacking one small box some familiar items appeared. The box contained the funeral programs of Great-Grandmother Mamie Atkinson (Grandpa Emmanuel, husband); Grandmother Janie (Grandpa Louis, Husband); Mom, and Chelly's second daughter (Destiny); she was only one month old. I walked out of the bedroom and sat down next to Michelle. Of course, we talked about the goodness of God down through the years.

Finally, the late-night hour had arrived. We stopped working but not talking. Michelle had endless questions about Bible characters. We discussed Bible doctrines and eschatological meanings. Her greatest interest focused on the Rapture of the church. She got her Bible and started highlighting passages of Scriptures.

Suddenly, it occurred to me that we were having a church service. The Holy Spirit was in our midst because there were two gathered together in His name (Matthew 18:20)! I was contented to answer every question as thoroughly as possible. We fellowshipped until 11:00 P.M., Chelly wanted me to stay until morning. I wanted to remain, but a malfunctioning car window precluded me from doing so. We prayed together for the last time. Michelle Lynn said, "Glenn, if the Rapture takes place tonight, I'm ready!" We embraced. I heard the priceless words, "Glenn, I love you" for the last time.

Unexpectedly *Unspeakable*

The next day, as we travelled back to Columbus this thought entered my mind going through Lodi, "I don't know what I would do without Chelly." We arrived home safely that night. The next day began as usual. The children headed to school and parents commuted to work. Around 10:30 A.M., a call was transferred to me. It was my mother-in-law. She was crying hysterically. She wanted me to leave my office and call her back when I was alone. Her breathing was so sporadic it was difficult to understand. "Please," I insisted. "Tell me right now!" The next words left me speechless and in shock! "Chelly is dead!" That's not possible, impossible! I said, "I just saw my sister less than 24 hours ago!" "What do you mean, she is dead!" Stunned, I asked, "How?" Still crying uncontrollably, my mother-in-law said, "In a car accident!"

I staggered out of the office. Wandering outside our office building, it occurred to me that I didn't drive today. I took the bus. Alone and in shock I rode a bus to my wife's job. I walked to her department. She took one look and said, "What's the matter!" My Chelly is gone. Unintelligibly, I stammered gibberish, "Someone hit Chelly; now, she's gone. I need to go, now, I need to see Chelly." We arrived at our newly built home. Our family had only lived in the house for five months. Chelly's family was going to come and spend the weekend with us.

I immediately walked into our bedroom closet and pulled the door closed. Prostrate I laid on the floor. This day O' Lord will I have words with thee!

> "Never before have I spoken to you in this capacity. I insist on knowing. Why? Two years ago, my mother died. And now, you have removed my only sister from this realm. Why? I vehemently protested! My brother and I have been evil men! She was a kind and affectionate woman. Bring her back and take me instead! Take me, now! Shall not the Righteous Judge of all the earth but answer me this one time?"

But the Lord did not speak to my spirit. He said nothing! I stood up and walked out of the closet. My wife was frantically packing. "No," I said. "Are we not staying overnight?" She asked. "No," I must go alone. I am not finished speaking to Him who called me to declare His Word. He and I will have words. Paula refused to move from the entrance. She probably stood there for thirty minutes pleading and reasoning. She was determined not to allow me to make this trip alone. "Glenn, you are emotionally unable to go anywhere," she said repeatedly. I merely responded, "He will answer me. He must. He must speak to me; He must." Finally, after what seemed like infinity, she stepped aside. Her angst and consternation were on full display. She was vehemently unhappy but stopped short of being a burden.

There was one central thought on my mind as I walked out of the house and got into the car. That thought engulfed me as the car door closed. The next three hours could only be described as a Shakespearean novel overlaid with scriptures from the book of Job. I remember my angry refrain, "Lord, my soul does indeed protest!" Why do the heathen rage! Murderers roam free. Rapists are pardoned. Pedophiles go unpunished. Corruption in the judicial system is rewarded. Fraudsters enrich themselves through Ponzi schemes. And radicalized terrorists bomb our children while studying in schools. Why have you allowed villainous, toilet bowl licking dogs to celebrate freely while the righteous perish? O' Lord, my broken soul does indeed protest! Repeatedly and in anguish, I asked why?

The sign read: Akron City Corporation Limits. I had been prayerfully agonizing for two hours. Deafening silence was my response. In that instant, a tingling numbness permeated my spirit like goose bumps. Déjà vu accurately describes that moment; that eerie moment when my wife informed me to go back to St. Elizabeth Medical Center. After making a U-turn on I-76, this is precisely what gripped my being. I was consumed by an emotional numbness that transcends any logical explanation.

Somehow my mind, body and spirit knew mom had transitioned; nevertheless, I couldn't accept it. Yes, that place, wherever that place is, I have been here before. Now, obviously, I am there again. It is the place between acceptance and denial. It is found between reality and surreality. The technical name for "spaces or intervals between" is called, *liminality*. Liminality is a term used in the study of anthropology (the study of human-kind). Liminality is the uncertainty or disorientation that occurs in the transition from one state to another. We'll discuss that term in greater detail in chapter nine, "Transition & Transformation." Whatever state I was in, it was mentally unhealthy. Suddenly, my phone rang. Again, Paula was calling to ensure my safety. It felt like she was calling every 30 minutes or so. Truthfully, I don't remember how frequently. I was busily searching for God. Where was He? I hadn't heard from Him since learning about the accident! God, why is this even happening? My brain was on vibrate. Nothing made sense. It felt like a horrible nightmare that refused to end! I needed to know why bad things happen to good people.

In the New York Times bestseller, "*When Bad Things Happen To Good People*," by Rabbi Harold S. Kushner, the question of why is thoroughly addressed. He writes,

"If the bad things that happened to us are a result of bad luck, and not the will of God," A woman asked me when the evening after I had delivered a lecture on my theology, "what makes bad luck happen?" I was stumped for an answer.

My instinctive response was that nothing makes bad luck happen; it just happens. But I suspected that there must be more to it than that. This is perhaps the philosophical idea which is the key to everything else I'm suggesting in this book. Can you accept the idea that somethings happen for no reason, that there is randomness in the universe? Some people cannot handle that idea. They look for connections, striving desperately to make sense of everything that happens. They convince themselves that God is cruel, or that they are simply unworthy sinners, rather than accept randomness. Sometimes, when people have made sense of 90% of everything, they assume that the remaining 10% will eventually make sense also. Making sense of everything, however, usually remains beyond human comprehension. So, why do we insist on everything being logical? Why must every occurrence be sensible, rational or happen for a specific reason? Why can't we let the universe have a few rough edges of randomness?

Why? That was the trillion-dollar question. I could not accept the universe's rough edges. I believed in pragmatics, logicalities and deductive reasoning. Randomness was not an alternative for me.

I needed specificity, rationality and concrete answers that provided sensible and judicious answers. I never subscribed to the belief that "all is relative."

In academia, it is known as intellectualization. You see, intellectualization works to reduce anxiety by thinking about events, especially, crisis in a clinical way. This defense mechanism allowed me to avoid the emotional aspect of the situation and instead, focus only on the intellectual component. Therefore, I needed to make sense of this randomness. How is it possible that my sister, a newly born-again, spirited-filled Woman of God could be killed in an indiscriminate automobile accident?

O' Spare Me, *that* I May Recover Strength
~ King David (Psalm 39:13)

Finally, I arrived at the condominium in Youngstown. I am not sure how I even got there. I just, got there. The trip was a blur of sorts. Thank God for his mercies. And yet, I still had this unsolved issue with the Maker. My nephew was playing outside by himself. Slowly, I walked toward him. Denzel was always quiet and introverted. He greeted me with these words, "Uncle Glenn, my mommy is dead." The definiteness of that statement was unnerving! I replied with as much poise as I could gather, "Yes. I know."

Tony greeted me as I entered. We talked for hours. Dessie, Chelly's husband was too distraught to discuss any details.

However, he did manage to share a story that was hauntingly familiar. "Glenn, I need to share something. Maybe you can give me an answer," he said. "I'll try, Dessie." I replied. Dessie stated that immediately after Chelly's accident, he left a message informing the pastor. The pastor, however, did not return the call. Dessie said, "I called a second time and left a message." In frustration he said, "All that money my wife gave to the church and I couldn't get a return phone call." He merely wanted prayer for himself and the children. The atmosphere intensified as he spoke. Finally, the pastor answered after two previous attempts. Grimacing as if in pain, Dessie continued, "The pastor said he was on a ladder painting and couldn't talk at this time." Dessie insisted that the funeral for his wife be held at her church. After listening to another familiar tale of awful pastoral leadership, I responded, "Dessie, the pastor's response was insensitive, shameless and irresponsible." I attempted to hide indignation, my exit from the room was swift. After entering the bedroom, I stared out the window in disbelief. Mom's pastor never called or visited. My sister's pastor was too busy to offer pastoral care for a family in grief. This was pastoral dereliction run amuck!

Before exiting the house, my brother shared a touching moment with me. He said, "Man we had some grand plans! The three of us were heading to Hawaii and the Grand Bahamas next year!" Anthony had been planning this for some time. Now, it would never happen.

Once again, I found myself in the untoward position of making homegoing arrangements for my sister at the same funeral home as mom in less than three years. Something snapped inside of me that day while leaving Chelly's condo. My eyes were opened. This event was neither covered in church bylaws nor constitutions. Church policy manuals, clergy guidelines, and departmental handbooks did not address the problem of emotional suffering. My theology was completely shattered. Never again would I view life the same, never. The false notion of perfectness with which I had viewed the world since accepting Christ was gone. Job said, "Man that is born of a woman is of few days, and full of trouble (14:1). James declared, "Whereas ye know not what shall be on the morrow. For what is life? It is even as a vapor, that appeareth for a little time, and then vanisheth away (4:14). King David, however, said it best, O' spare me that I may recover strength, before I go away and be no more. Life is filled with tragedies for which there are neither explanation nor understanding.

Life's Tragedy

It may be misery not to sing at all,
And to go silent through the brimming day;
It may be misery never to be loved,
But deeper griefs than these beset the way.
To sing the perfect song,
And by a half-tone lost the key,
There the potent sorrow, there the grief,
The pale, sad staring of Life's Tragedy.

~ Paul Lawrence Dunbar

This experience was very different from watching my mother's health slowly decline. Chelly was healthy. She was an exuberant wife and mother fully prepared to enjoy her life. I needed an answer. When I was unable to secure an acceptable answer; placing blame became a priority. Someone needed to be held accountable for this unacceptable tragedy. From my perspective there were numerous entities involved in this tragedy.

First, I was hurt that God did not prevent this from happening. Although, it was unfathomable to think that God was somehow responsible; nevertheless, He certainly could have prevented it. Secondly, my anger was directed toward the false prophets posturing in pulpits across America. Every Sunday, a smiling face promises health, wealth and prosperity to anyone who desires to become a Christian. These spiritual guides failed to prepare Christians for life's harsh realities. They would have us believe that tragedy is disallowed while serving God. Weekly, millions are told no sorrow, pain, agony, disappointment or unexplainable tragedy could happen while faithfully serving God.

Happy, happy, joy, joy was their Sunday morning refrain. Everyone displays miles and miles of billboard smiles. In one church service, Chelly and I heard, "Jesus is like a Snickers bar. He is satisfyingly delicious!" Huh? The Son of God is like peanuts and caramel covered in chocolate. Really?

Lastly, I charged a portion of this tragedy to manipulative people who enjoyed my sister's resources but despised her success. These devious, conniving schemers certainly played their part. My physical and emotional strength was gone. I was angry and exhausted. Unable to think rationally, pray meaningfully or worship truthfully, I just sat in the car and cried.

Tragedy is a disastrous event for everyone involved. Dr. H. Norman Wright, author of *The Complete Guide to Crisis & Trauma Counseling* explains:

> "All persons have a definite subsequent reaction on hearing the bad news. The first phase of a crisis is the impact phase, which is usually very brief. For some people, it is like being hit with a two-by-four. It is becoming aware of the crisis and experiencing the effect of being stunned. This period lasts from a few hours to a few days, depending upon the event and the person involved. In a severe loss, tears can occur immediately or a few days later.

The more severe the crisis or loss, the greater the impact and the greater the amount of incapacitation and numbness. During this impact stage, we are usually less competent than normal, and our usual tendency of handling life's problems will probably emerge. If, however, your tendencies are rooted in avoidance, it is most likely that you are going to run. However, fighting in attempting to take charge during a crisis seems to be the healthier response. And because each of the succeeding phases is dependent upon the adjustments made in the previous one, avoiding reality does not make for good judgment. Pain is prolonged instead of resolved."

Dr. H. Norman Wright identifies four phases associated with a normal crisis pattern.

1. Phase I   Impact
2. Phase II   Withdrawal Confusion
3. Phase III   Adjustment
4. Phase IV   Reconstruction/Reconciliation

1. Impact: The first phase of a crisis the impact phase, which is usually very brief. During the impact stage, our thinking capability is lessened.
2. Withdrawal Confusion: During the second phase, the tendency to deny one's feelings is probably stronger than at any other phase. Intense anger occurs toward whatever happened, which in some cases brings forth guilt for having such feelings.
3. Adjustment: The third phase of a crisis is the adjustment phase, which takes longer than others. The emotional responses during this time are hopeful.
4. Reconstruction: A characteristic of this phase is the spontaneous expression of hope. There is a sense of confidence – plans are made out of this sense of confidence.

Other professionals define crisis in stages as opposed to phases. However, the terminology is quite similar:

1. **Shock stage**: Initial paralysis at hearing the bad news
2. **Denial stage**: Mental avoidance, resisting the obvious
3. **Anger stage**: Frustration and intense emotional display
4. **Displacement stage**: Someone is responsible
5. **Depression stage**:   Final realization of the inevitable
6. **Acceptance stage**:   Finally progressing forward

The danger for anyone going through crisis is that they may become stuck at in a certain stage. For example, while in denial, an individual may be unwilling to accept reality. The inevitable future of acceptance is never materialized. That is, the person who has lost their job still gets dressed, commutes to a public place near the former employer like a library or park and remains there until the work-shift ends. Other issues while in crisis include individuals that move on to the next phase but did not satisfactorily complete an earlier phase.

Therefore, they move back-and-forth in emotional stages. Arguably, the pre-final stage of depression is often considered the most complicated because it renders one vulnerable to debilitation. Debilitation impairs holistic strength. Holistic refers to the whole person. If in fact, we are trichotomous, which means divided into three parts; we are comprised of mind (psyche/emotions), body (physical) and (spirit). Crisis situations tend to deplete energy in every area of our holistic being. Crisis can make people vulnerable, even the best of us are subject to the influence of tragedy and crisis. Yes, crisis has the potential to make strong men weep, wise women irrational, business leaders irresponsible and thoughtful people insensitive. Often, whatever is perceived during a crisis quickly becomes reality. It doesn't matter if it is nonsensical or completely irrational. Whatever is perceived as real, becomes real. "For as he thinketh in his heart so is he .... (Proverbs 23:7).

The next few days felt as if I were standing at the top of the smoky mountains somewhere in Gatlinburg, Tennessee. Preparation for Chelly's homegoing service was painfully familiar. Nevertheless, I was able to prepare the entire program with God's help. Of course, Dessie asked me to serve as eulogist. I consented. Unlike mom's funeral, I don't remember the details preceding my sister's funeral service. The only details I can recall after saying goodbye to Anthony and walking out of Chelly's condominium was, helping dad purchase a suit, shirt and tie for the funeral. I distinctly remember Tom crying while trying the suit on for size. I also remember feeling powerless to help him. My only other memory of that week was arriving at the church moments before the funeral service searching for a parking space.

The rest of the week is a blur of nothingness. I don't recollect names, places, events or spiritual experiences. I just kept wondering where was God in all of this? The funeral service was extraordinarily crowded. There weren't enough seats for the friends and guests. It was standing room only in a building capable of easily seating 300.

I remember walking into the sanctuary wearing a minister's robe and caring a Bible. Alone and empty are the words to best describe my emotional state of being. I never knew pain could feel this way. My mind was numb, voices were inaudible, and everything seemed as if it were moving in slow motion.

People were understandably remorseful, grief stricken and openly sobbing while others appeared dazed in disbelief. The pulpit seemed like a football field away. Perhaps this was some form of psychological disorientation, but the moment seemed surreal. Dear God, is that really my Chelly in a casket? Is this really happening? There was an inclination to just disrobe and run as far away as possible. As the long journey toward the pulpit was ending, someone stood up to embrace me. She was in such pain. Whatever virtue I possessed prior to that moment was gone. That person extracted the limited residual. There was nothing remaining, nothing.

Then, suddenly he came. Like Jesus suddenly materialized after walking through a solid wall to show Thomas a pair of nail scarred hands; the presence of the Holy Spirit expressed an instantaneous and overwhelming love. It happened without me even making a conscious effort to pray. I wanted to ask Him, where have you been? Job, like me, wondered, God, where were you? But Job was rebuked for questioning God about the lack of intervention during His servant's personal crisis.

God asked Job a few rhetorical questions. "Who is this that obscures my plans with words without knowledge? Brace yourself like a man; I will question you, and you shall answer me. Where were you when I laid the earth's foundation?

Tell me, if you understand. Who marked off its dimensions? Surely you know! Who stretched a measuring line across it? On what were its footings set, or who laid its cornerstone—while the morning stars sang together, and all the angels shouted for joy?" (Job 38:2-7 NIV).

The strength of God's Spirit undergirded me in route to the pulpit. By the time I knelt to pray, His presence provided an assurance without which spiritual undertakings are not possible, especially eulogizing your only sister. The serenity of the Holy Spirit became a spiritual sedative for me. My father in Christ, Bishop Norman L. Wagner entered the sanctuary. He took the seat next to me.

As I stood to minister, God's Spirit enveloped me. I watched my beloved's casket slowly close. I should have experienced grief beyond description. Instead, I experienced the meaning of God's Holy Word, "Behold, I am with always, even until the end..." (Matthew 28:20). I don't remember the title of the sermon nor its contextual theme or homiletical style. I do, however, remember leading the procession out of the sanctuary. I don't remember going to the graveyard. I cannot recall any aspect of the interment service whatsoever. Perhaps, I had experienced the defense mechanism called, repression. And in that case, perhaps it worked for my own good.

He Heals *the* Broken Hearted & Binds Up Their Wounds
~ Psalms 147:3

Psalmist Marvin Sapp declared, "Never would have made it without you. I would have lost it all, but now I see that you were there for me." Never a truer statement was ever made about my state of being. My great-grandmother often sang, "If it had not been for the Lord on my side, tell me where would I be, where would I be!" I would most likely be dead or doing 25–to– life in a maximum federal prison without chance of parole. Life has peaks and valleys. Learning how to worship God when on top is as important. However, it is no less important than learning how to worship God when you are on the bottom. Therefore, whether on top or bottom, learning how to live in submission to His will is paramount. But I was still struggling with learning how to live in submission to His will in an unexpected traumatic crisis.

Again, I have no memories of the aftermath. Memories of the trip back to Columbus are nonexistent. All that mattered, Chelly was no longer here. I was feeling some kind of way about it! I knew my life would never be the same. And yet, the agony of an unexplainable event remained stuck in my mind like a splinter in my very soul. I just needed everything to make sense. Therefore, emotions needed to be removed from the equation. Rationality was my post-crisis resolution.

Emotions became an internal enemy. Emotionality fostered mental instability. Emoting was disallowed. Logic became my default template. Deductive reasoning was the compass for navigating life. I despised any form of weakness, especially in men. Pragmatic Christianity became the Walter marque. My mental attitude was stoic and hard like Chromium! Chromium is the hardest metal known to man. That was my new brand, Chromium man. Future forward, intellectualizing was the sole means for obtaining resolution.

No, It Doesn't *Go Away* But Recovery Is Possible

What seemed like years really amounted to only about six months. I lived in a perpetual state of grief. Playfulness had been officially evicted from my life. Every day I asked the same questions. Every day I found a new place to cry. There would be no calling off from work. All my professional responsibilities were met. Each Sunday my family faithfully attended worship services. There would be no sending the children to church. We worshipped together. Afterwards, we arrived home and ate as a family. Later, our children played with their friends. My wife busied herself preparing for work. Me, I stared out the window. I hated Sunday afternoons! Sunday afternoons were for weekly phone calls to check on mom and Chelly. I was intensely angry. The anger, however, was psychologically exhausting. Intellectualizing was a rational alternative. Unfortunately, intellectualizing made things worse! John W. James and Russell Friedman co-authored *The Grief Recovery Handbook*. In the handbook, the issue of intellectualizing grief is addressed. James and Friedman writes,

> "The attempt to shift from emotions to intellect is a dangerous and counterproductive thing to do with grieving people. Grief is, by definition, the emotional response to loss. The cause of the loss itself is intellectual, but the reaction to it is emotional. That's not to say there is anything wrong with using our minds, but where is it

written that we can't employ both intellect and emotions when they're called for? One of humanity's great gifts is the ability to demonstrate and communicate emotions. Yet society seems to place negative value on this gift. Our reliance on intellect at the expense of feelings has reached epidemic proportions – particularly where grief is concerned. One reason is that the death of a loved one is not an everyday occurrence. It is not surprising that people approach emotional pain intellectually. Since we rely on our minds every day, we're far more practiced at using them."

In retrospect, intellectualizing prohibited me from going through the normal grief phases/stages. A pathway back to worship was critically needed. Please note, I did not say that a pathway back to church services, choir rehearsals, community outreach gatherings, conventions or state councils was needed. A pathway back to God through worship was the only spiritual therapeutic remedy for my grieving soul. This is a good place to define grief. According to James and Friedman, "grief is the conflicting feelings caused by the end of or change in a familiar pattern of behavior." Every human being experiences grief. In this regard grief is natural. Perhaps more importantly, grief is an important biblical concept. The Word of God exclaims that Christians should not grieve as if we are hopeless.

"But we do not want you to be uninformed, brethren, about those who are asleep, so that you will not grieve as do the rest who have no hope" (1 Thessalonians 4:13 NAS).

Certified Grief Recovery Specialist, Bishop F. Josephus Johnson II, author of *Grief, A Biblical Pathway to God*, explains,

> "On the other hand, if we as believers have been growing in Jesus Christ, we have experienced thousands of reasonable encounters, in emotive context, where Jesus comes through for us. These encounters form a principle of hope in our core beliefs. When difficult situations arise, we know without reasoning or thinking about it, that Jesus is going to come and help us out. We have hope that God will straighten things out now, or in the resurrection. Therefore, we do not grieve as those who have no hope, because hope tempers our grief. We do hurt and struggle through grief, but there is a supernatural element of hope that is mixed with our heart and struggle!

So, grief is an important biblical concept and we experience that grief differently from those who do not have Jesus Christ." Every crisis is very different. Worship happens during crisis but in various forms. Not every experience is the same. My worshipful experience with mom was totally different than with Chelly.

I had to reconcile my heart with the reality that Chelly was no longer present in this dimension. Truthfully, I did not blame God, but my heart moaned because He could have prevented it. Nevertheless, this worship experience taught me not to confuse the will of God with the abilities of God!

Velvet Wrapped In Steel

Michelle Lynn Walter was merely a gift God chose to share with you for only a limited time. Of all the families on earth that she could have belonged to, God chose to share her with you. But make no mistake, she belonged to God. She was an instrument of His glory reflected on earth!

~ Pastor Marie

He could have prevented it; He chose to allow it. I will never understand that decision. But the clay is never going to understand the Potter. It took some time, but I have learned to say it is well with my soul. Early one morning, a loving friend explained God's divine providence in terms that I'll always remember.

"Your sister was merely a gift God chose to share with you for only a limited time. Of all the families on earth that she could have belonged to, God chose to share her with you. But make no mistake, she belonged to God. She was an instrument of His glory reflected on earth!

Chelly was Chromium wrapped in velvet! She was beautiful and tough as steel! God exhaled and released her from heaven into the earthly realm through Tom and Diane. He inhaled – and her spirit returned back to the Creator of Life. Her essence will forever be a part of my journey. And, if I live right I shall see her again.

For as it is written, "But I would not have you to be ignorant, brethren, concerning them which are asleep, that ye sorrow not, even as others which have no hope. For if we believe that Jesus died and rose again, even so them also which sleep in Jesus will God bring with him. For this we say unto you by the word of the Lord, that we which are alive and remain unto the coming of the Lord shall not prevent them which are asleep. For the Lord himself shall descend from heaven with a shout, with the voice of the archangel, and with the trump of God: and the dead in Christ shall rise first: Then we which are alive and remain shall be caught up together with them in the clouds, to meet the Lord in the air: and so shall we ever be with the Lord. Wherefore comfort one another with these words" (1 Thessalonians 4:14-18).

Worshipping *Through* Reconciliation

My father and I had a strained relationship for most of our lives. However, God, in His divine providence saved the best years for last. My dad took many odd jobs trying to ensure our well-being. My father's work ethic was faultless. He worked extraordinarily hard. Tom was many things, but laziness could never be attributed to him. I need to provide an overview of Walter family's history. The complex dynamics of our relationship is inextricably connected to dad's family. And yes, there were social, environmental and educational factors. Tom's upbringing, however, was undisputedly the most influential factor in our relationship. Of course, salvation and worship will eventually take center stage in this relationship but not until the later stages of life. Let me explain.

Take Me Back *to the* Place Where I First Believed

Dad was born in Birmingham, Alabama, on February 2, 1941 at exactly 6:00 P.M., with the aid of an experienced midwife. He was the second youngest of 10 children, eight sons (Chuck, Howard, Luellen, (Willa Mae) William, Gus, Nathaniel, Ned, Tommy (Rosa Lee) and two daughters. After his birth, Tommy's parents Willie Walter and Lucy Atkins-Walter moved to Browns, Alabama. After the death of Willie, Tommy and his siblings were raised by his grandparents Gus and Fanny Walter Great-grandpa Gus owned 100 acers of farm property that included cows, mules, chickens and various crops.

I did not know my great grandparents or grandparents on dad's side. However, I had a personal relationship with every uncle and aunt. I knew each of them very well. My aunts possessed every measure of southern hospitality and charm. They epitomized gracefulness. However, Dad's brothers were nuts!

My mom being a northern socialite of the debutante sort, regularly reminded me of that fact. She routinely said, "All of Tom's brothers should be committed to the state." Her soprano voice carried the loftiness of Rayen High School's lead majorette, "Something is wrong with each of them." Of course, I loved them! They were grimy rascals. They were military officers, law enforcement officers, housing construction workers, GM plant supervisors, Wean United Steel workers, and et cetera. Uncle William, whom I lived with for a period of my life, lived in Los Angeles. He owned a liquor store, gasoline station, strip mall, shoe store and car wash. He was worth a mountain pile of money. But Uncle Chuck was worth much more. William's house would have fit inside Chuck's home. He owned a fleet of semi-trucks. His transportation company was in Chicago. He was a wealthy trucking industrialist. He started it during the 70s.

That's not bad for a Black man in America. Each one was professionally respected. My uncles worked hard, played hard and lived hard! I attribute my work ethic and love of global travel to my father and uncles.

At the invitation of Uncle William, Tom left Birmingham at the age of 16 and traveled with a friend, John Lamb (Sharon Line-McGuffey Heights, Youngstown), who provided transportation to Youngstown, Ohio. Upon arriving, an entry level position at The Penn-Ohio Coat, Apron, & Towel Supply Co. located on North Avenue in Youngstown, awaited.

One day, while relaxing in his brother's home (Gus) who also lived on North Avenue not far from the Towel Supply Co., Tom noticed a charming young lady walking by the factory either to visit her grandparents, Emmanuel and Mamie Atkinson, who resided across the street from the factory (410 North Avenue) or on the way home. She was the lead majorette of The Rayan High School. As God would have it, Tommy's brother, Gus, named after their grandfather, knew the charming student's cousin, Barbara Jean. Tommy was introduced to mom in 1961, and soon thereafter, Tommy and Diane Marie were married in 1962. For a brief period, they resided with Diane's parents Louis and Janie Cobb at 255 Carlton Street. In October, Diane gave birth to yours truly, at North Side Hospital.

In 1964, Dad and Mom moved to Brooklyn, New York. Tom worked in a large bakery located in New Jersey. Although they enjoyed living in New York, they returned to Ohio after nearly two years. Dad began working at the Ohio Chair Company located on Mahoning Avenue in 1966. He enjoyed playing for the company softball team, the Ohio Chair All-stars.

Later that year, the couple moved into McGuffey Terrace. It was a beautiful ground level two-bedroom apartment. In 1967, the couple welcomed Anthony. Again, Tom searched for an opportunity to increase the family's quality of life. He found it at Wonder Bread Company located at 1535 Mahoning Avenue. However, due to unforeseen economic events, the young family had to make temporary quarters with Mom's grandparents in 1968. In 1969, William, now a business owner and resident of Los Angles, California, invited Tom to join him and make a life for his family on America's west coast. Always an opportunist, Tom resigned from Wonder Bread and joined his brother in Los Angles.

In early 1970, Dad sent for mom to join him in Los Angles, California. Great–grandma Mamie and grandma Janie insisted that my brother and I remain with them. Great–grandma Mamie was the family matriarch. She was God's woman–in–charge. She was a worshipper! I once saw her stand between my mother and a madman with a gun in his hand. I'll never forget her words.

She calmingly stated, "Put that gun down." She confidently walked between the man with the pointed gun and my mother. As she positioned herself in front of mom, she said, "Before you get to her, you must go through me. And before you go through me, you must go through God!"

The man lowered the gun and left our house. I watched that entire encounter. Please understand, her word was law! Thurgood Marshall and the U.S. Supreme Court could not overturn *her* rulings. She informed my parents that they needed to get properly settled. Afterwards, they could come and get us. I didn't just learn about the great women of the Bible, I lived with the great women of the New Testament Church. I was raised by worshippers!

Tom and Diane found an apartment in Compton. It was a lovely stucco apartment located on Compton Boulevard close to Rosecrans Avenue. The family lived in Compton for only a brief time. On October 3, 1970, Diane gave birth to their third child, Michelle (Chelly) Lynn. Princess Chelly was born in St Elizabeth hospital. After Michelle's birth, Tommy returned to Los Angles. He intended to relocate his entire family to the Greater Los Angeles area. He worked with William's conglomerate of business for over one year.

However, in 1972, Great–grandma Mamie purchased a magnificent home located at 135 Breaden Street. The house served as residence for four generations of family. Mamie stated that no member of her family would ever be without a place to live. This huge three-story home came with a two-car garage and a large back yard. It also contained a lower level that included three bedrooms, a kitchen with cabinetry & eatery, bathroom with shower and laundry area facilities.

The main floor boasted of living, dining, and family rooms, as well as, a traditional sit–in kitchen. The second level was comprised of four bedrooms including a single living suite. The third level was a separate studio scale living quarter. On November 7, 1972, my mother and I began painting the second level bedrooms prior to moving in. This purchase was a significant event because the death of Diane's father, grandmother, and mother all occurred within a brief period of three years.

In spring 1973, Tom permanently returned to Youngstown. He had come a long way from the back roads of Browns, Alabama. Tom arrived with a large savings and a new luxury car (Cadillac Coup Deville) for which he paid cash. He immediately began working at General Motors' Fisher Auto Body, located in Lordstown, Ohio. He remained an employee of GM until downsizing began in 1976.

By then, I was a young active teenager but by no means typical. My generational work ethic was now evident in me as well. Government welfare programs were never an option. No excuses for lack of effort. My work habits were concretely resolute. A new philosophical framework began formulating in my soul: dream it, plan it, and achieve it. My heart was that of a hardhat blue-collar worker, but my mind was idealistically white-collar thinker.

As a teenager, it became obvious that God gives no man greatness but instead, He would give him the ability with which to achieve it. My mother knew I had the ability to achieve. She consistently spoke to the achiever in me. Dad, however, spoke to the neighborhood desperado. He did not possess the empathic aptitude to interpersonally connect.

Retrospectively, I realize that Tom's giftedness was in his ability to physically work through calamity. He was neither intuitive nor overly communicative. Rural Alabama did not afford him that social convenience. Thus, Tom and I lacked a father and son closeness. By age 12, my name was already appearing in the Youngstown Vindicator. Each Sunday, I hurried to get Sunday's paper from the porch. I immediately looked for the Volley Rogers youth Football section in the Sports Section. I loved reading, of course, about me. I'd cut out my quarterback (QB) exploits and paste them on my wall. Ah, yes, I would be the next Bob Griese.

I liked the Miami Dolphin QB because he and I had something in common. We both threw touchdown passes and wore glasses. That's about all we had in common. He was a rich and famous NFL QB on the front cover of Sporting News Magazine. And I was, well, not rich and famous. And, I was never mentioned in Sporting News Magazine, like ever.

Tom and I didn't have so–called "bonding moments." He worked hard and played hard but not with his family. We grew ever distant. Dad did not attend my functions.

He was not involved in school activities. Tom visited my school in the first grade. He paid for a box of (unsold) chocolate candy bars while in the sixth grade. He attended the 12th grade musical production of Lil' Abner. He didn't attend sporting banquets or academic award ceremonies. He never saw me throw a touchdown. He never heard my name called during high school award ceremonies. To his credit, Tom did make the high school graduation ceremony. Actually, mom made him come to the graduation but to his credit, he agreed.

After securing a CDL license, Dad took pride in driving for a regional trucking company. Again, however, because of the ominous economic conditions throughout Mahoning County, drivers were scaled down and Tommy was released. Nevertheless, true to his modus operandi, he quickly landed on his feet and secured another job with Youngstown Public Schools. Tom enjoyed working for the department of transportation driving buses.

I listened to his adventurous tales whenever visiting home while on break. During this time, Tom returned to the foundation of his grandfather's faith. He and Mom attended the services of Zion Apostolic Church located on Belmont Avenue, where District Elder Charles Scott served as pastor. During the revival services, Tom gave his life to Christ and was filled with the Holy Spirit.

Finally, he was taken back to the faith of his childhood. He went back before the custom silk suits by Lord Chesterfield. He went back before the multiple Cadillac Coup De Villes. He went back to the place where he first believed! My mom shared the great news with me. As it happened to be, I was scheduled to be in Youngstown the following day. After arriving, Tom and I talked at great length about his conversion to Christ. He was genuinely sincere about serving the Lord. But like Lot of the Old Testament, Tom's righteous soul was soon vexed by an unhealthy environment and unrighteous associates. It doesn't matter how well-meaning converts are. After conversion, born again believers are subject to make mistakes because they are still spiritual babes. That is, they are new to spiritual warfare. Our adversary, the devil is extraordinarily crafty at misdirection, deceitfulness and catering to our old carnal appetites.

It is imperative that all newly born-again believers quickly get away from old and familiar places. In other words, lay aside every – weight – thing that so easily entangles us (Hebrews 12:1). Please note the specificity of wording. The Bible says, "easily" entangles. The author of Hebrews uses a compound Greek word which derived from *eu – periistemi*. It is transliterated in English as *Euperistatos*. It describes what is literally encompassing or encircling. It denotes something that prevents or retards running. It encircles someone who desperately needs to advance. The word is found in the Bible only once.

It's never too late to be Transformed…

Unfortunately, Dad did not regularly attend spiritual related activities (worship services, Bible classes, Christian social events) neither did the people in his personal circle. In fact, it was only a matter of time until the new Tom became an old familiar figure, except he was worse. Dad became an estranged member of the family. His disaffection had a minimal impact on me. Three generations of prayerful worshippers covered and protected me. My brother and sister, however, felt maximum impact. Tom's untoward decision, as do the decisions of every leader, affects everyone under the span of his or her influence. Dad's decision to turn away from Christ had enormous impact. Tom did things to my brother that he would have never thought about doing to me. My great–grandparents would have run him out of Ohio. He made comments to Mom and Chelly that are not worthy of repeating.

For years, the Walter family functioned as an entity of four. Our immediate family remained that way until my siblings and I were adults with our own families. During Dad and Mom's empty nest phase, Diane's health began deteriorating. Tom displayed every sign of Cognitive Dissonance. He wanted to be a supportive Christian husband but couldn't overcome an inconsistent tendency to avoid situations that made him uncomfortable.

Dad was physically present most of the time but emotionally absent all the time. He just could not emotionally connect with his wife, children or grandchildren. For example, it had been years since I left home. Tom never called to check on the well-being of my children. For that matter, he never called to say hello. After years of experiencing his emotional disconnection, my siblings and I simply stopped trying. Tom lived in a world of continual or perpetual detachment. He was the stiff choir member unable to sway in unison. He could not feel the groove of rhythmic movement. Tom reminded me of the cadet at basic training who was unable to march in unison with the squadron. Dad needed a mathematical genius to write an algorithm for interpersonal relations.

We kept Tom at a distance after Mom transitioned. Chelly was the group harmonizer. She reminded us of Mom's tender loving kindness. But in less than three years, Chelly was gone. The after-effects were horrific! Now, Anthony and I were faced with a morally dichotomous dilemma. Find a way to reconcile with Tom or live in the aftermath of disconnection and anger. Anthony made an immediate and unapologetic choice. I felt the same way as Tony. But the thing about Christianity – until your theology comes out of the Bible and is practiced, it's not real. And the best example of applied theology is changed behavior. Soon, God would provide an opportunity for me to help Tom.

His Eye 𝄞 On The Sparrow

It is impossible to help someone without getting involved in their struggle. Tom wanted to make amends. He worked diligently every day for the next three years as a grandfather. Tom vowed to raise Chelly's only daughter, Tierra DaShawn. With Anthony's support, they moved into an apartment in Boardman, Ohio. Anthony provided years of financial support which enabled Tierra to attend school and participate in extra–curricular activities, especially track and field. Tommy decided, however, to raise Tierra in a different environment far from the familiarity of Youngstown. My brother had done his part to reconcile. Now, it was my turn.

Tom decided to move to Los Angeles. After their initial arrival in LA, Tom moved in with his brother William. After one year, Tom and Tierra, found an ideal studio apartment in Long Beach, California. I traveled to LA to assist with the move. God was unquestionably working on my behalf. We were able to secure every piece of furniture without expending any money! We enrolled Tierra in Compton High School. I became intricately involved with Tierra's high school exploits. Ms. Heather Hodgson (Guidance Counselor) often conferred with me on major and minor matters pertaining to Tierra's education. I knew if my niece was late to school, missed a class or did anything to jeopardize her graduating.

Early one morning, Tierra called me crying. She wanted to know why her life had been turned upside down. I listened very attentively. We talked for a lengthy time. Then, God opened the door. "Uncle Glenn, I want the Lord to come into my heart." She continued, "I want His Spirit to come inside of me!" That was my cue to minister. The Father was knocking on her heart and she invited Him in. As a minister, my job warranted that I properly introduce Tierra to Christ. It's what ministers do. I prayed for my niece. Then, the phone dropped. She was no longer listening to me. She was having a private conversation with her Heaven Father. I couldn't understand the discussion because it was taking place in a heavenly language that I didn't comprehend. The Psalmist said, a constant friend is He; His eye is on the sparrow and I know he watches me! So, I sang because I was happy. I sang because my Sister's daughter was free. His eye is on the sparrow, and I know He watches her and He watches me!

With God's help, Tierra graduated. I attended the graduation ceremony. Tom, with the help of his sons, had successfully honored his commitment. Tom loved Tierra the way he should have loved Chelly. After graduation, Tierra forwent an opportunity to attend Compton Community College and Long Beach State University. Instead, she returned to Youngstown in preparation for her wedding. The following year, came with two somewhat unsettling events.

First, Tierra sent her younger brother Dessie to Long Beach to be parented by Tom. And, although he endeavored to take care of Dessie, health and financial challenges prevented that from occurring. Second, William became ill and unexpectedly died. Dad asked me to help. Again, I was asked to help with making the final arrangements for one of my uncles. I had just eulogized Aunt Rosa Lee.

Immediately after William's interment, I facilitated yet another move. This move would transfer Tom to his brother Nathaniel, a resident of Birmingham, Alabama. He was happy to bring in the New Year with Nathaniel. Tom lived with "Nate" for a very brief period. I assisted Tom with moving into the historical Freedom Manor Senior Citizens Tower. This historical site was one block from the landmark 16th Street Baptist Church, directly across from the Civil Rights Park and less than one block from Birmingham Civil Rights Institute. Tommy was very pleased to once again be in a city where a sibling resided.

During a visit in June, Dad and I viewed the site where Black men, women, and even children as young as six years old were attacked by dogs and sprayed with water hoses. During my visit on this occasion, Tom began to reminiscence about Friday, September 13, 1963, when he and his young wife along with their first born, one-year old baby, was visiting family in Birmingham, Alabama.

Tom 22, and Mom 17, spent Saturday visiting his sister, Willa Mae. However, on Sunday, September 15th, 1963, he and Diane

were driving only blocks away from the Sixteenth Street Baptist Church, where the early morning bomb exploded. After sharing this story, Tom repeated a familiar refrain: "I miss Diane." He said, "I often hear her telling me what to do." I held back tears. God was softening Tom's heart. It was only a matter of time.

Prior to my departure, Tom asked, "When do you complete your doctor's degree?" What was this, Tom expressing an interest in my graduation? I said, "Prayerfully, I'll finish in six months." He replied' "I want to come!" Tom kept that promise. It took him 40 years to celebrate a measure of my academic success. Mom would have been proud!

Tom immeasurably enjoyed the company of Nate. The brothers often ate breakfast together and spent entire days fishing. They also attended church services. Tom especially enjoyed Sunday school. His time with Nathaniel, unlike William however, would be very short lived. Nathaniel passed within two years after Dad's arrival. As with William's passing, Tom asked me to be present. Tom's grief was more intense than any of his previous brothers.

After Nathaniel's death, Tom was hospitalized with pneumonia. Upon his release, several neighbors helped with his home care. I encouraged his recovery by promising to bring Tierra and her daughter Mierra for a visit at the end of the summer. After their visit concluded, Tom's niece Annie Jones, the daughter of Willa Mae pleaded for her uncle to remain in Birmingham, but he longed to be closer to his family and the surroundings of Ohio. God was reeling him in.

In Transition ℀ Transformation

Once again, Dad asked for my help to make the journey back to the Midwestern United States. I agreed. My spirit was telling me. This was my last opportunity to help dad make his calling and election sure. At 70, dad still had the strength to move furniture. It was his southern work ethic. We moved all the furniture down four stories using multiple elevators, including an exquisite bedroom suite into a moving van. We drove nine hours through a snow storm across four states. Mom would have been very pleased. Chelly would have said, "Glenn, get to the airport right now and leave Tom in Alabama!" Then, she would have waited for me to call from the airport with a flight number.

Dad's new residence was a picturesque and spacious apartment in Columbus, Ohio. Tom was very pleased. I visited weekly.

He regularly attended church services at the Church of Christ of The Apostolic Faith where he was re-baptized in Jesus' name six years prior to returning. Soon after settling, dad began to experience some physical challenges that resulted in multiple bouts with pneumonia and subsequent hospitalizations.

After being released from Mt. Carmel West, I arranged for an occupation therapist, physical therapist and a social worker to provide special care for my father. In addition to those specialists, food services were contracted to bring Tom's meals daily. Nevertheless, he became discontented. Tommy, always an independent person would routinely venture out to purchase items from the local grocers. On several occasions however, emergency squads were required to assist him getting home.

Closure ℅ Forever...

Finally, it was time. I sat with Tom and had the talk. Dad was determined to make everyone cater to his demands. I expressed 40 years of anguish and frustration with a man who was determined to make others sacrifice for his contentment. I never stopped honoring him throughout this discussion, but I had enough. "Dad, Mom died without your daily involvement in her medical treatment plan. My sister died with a complex about her appearance. My brother left home because he was afraid to sleep at night."

From that introduction an hour long narrative ensued. He wept like a child when we finished talking. He asked for forgiveness. Sobbing, he said, "Son, if I could go back…" I interrupted. "Dad, it's too late to go back! However, it's not too late to move forward." With that conversation, closure occurred for me. Closure, however, did not happen for Tom Walter. He simply refused to comply with the therapist's rehabilitative regiment. Tom was masterful in the arts of manipulation. Although he never read Machiavelli, he used cunning savvy to get others to do his bidding including purchasing products counterproductive to his own good. Of course, his imported pleasures were confiscated by yours truly. I informed his neighbors that there would be consequences for aiding and abetting. Eventually, Tom grew tired of my interference with his self–inflicting harmful practices.

One day, I entered the building collected Tom's mail and proceeded to the apartment. Astonishingly, Tom was gone! Later that morning, I discovered that Tierra and husband, Michael drove to Columbus and facilitated Tom's unannounced return to the city he loved, Youngstown, Ohio.

Tom Walter was blissful while residing with Tierra and Michael. He insisted on being independent although nearly setting their kitchen on fire while cooking. He was truly delighted to be reunited with his granddaughter, but grandpa was soon hospitalized with pneumonia.

He was required to undergo six-weeks of rigorous rehabilitative therapy. Unfortunately, Tom's health continued to decline.

God Is In *The* Details

His rehabilitation was not successful. I noticed a sharp decline in dad's physical motor skills. Tom began experiencing disequilibrium. Walking short distances soon became problematic without assistance. The last time my father walked unassisted was during the Thanksgiving holiday. My mind began recalling the horrid details of Diane's amputation during Thanksgiving, as I watched him walk the corridor.

As Tom set down to eat, I saw the food on his plate, but it reminded me of Diane's last meal prior to my departure from St. Elizabeth's Hospital. In that incident, I sincerely doubted that my father would ever again enjoy independent living. I left that rehabilitative center with an eerie feeling of déjà vu. I had visited this place twice before. It's that place between acceptance and denial. Well, there I was again standing in the intersection of *liminality* – the interval between leaving and arriving. This was my third mental journey to the zone between reality and surreality. That's when I knew. I knew that my father was dying. My time with him was rapidly concluding.

Over the next six months three major events transpired. First, dad became a permanent resident of the rehabilitative center. Secondly, Tierra, who was acting as primary contact, moved from Youngstown and took residence in Alabama. Lastly, Anthony and I became primary and secondary legal agents (Attorney-in-fact) of our father's affairs. We possessed the durable and health care power(s) of attorney for dad. We became intricately involved in every aspect of Tom's life. Anthony and I managed everything from the quality of Tom's mattress to the brand of insulin for his daily injections. We knew more about dad's medical information than he did. I knew every staff member by name. And believe me; they knew me as Dr. Walter, Tommy's son! I was praying that the favor of God would help me manage the details. "God, please get in the details!" I prayed for the physical strength and mental acuity to be a blessing. If you ever want to be a blessing to someone's life during a crisis, learn to pray for divine favor. Trust me; you are going to need God to help you manage the details.

The next year can only be described as bonding and eternal preparation. My brother and I alternated visiting Tom with such frequency that we knew what station his television was on. My visits with Tom were God–given uninterrupted church services consisting of explanation of Bible concepts, confessionals and demonstrations of love. Dad did not like being in this facility, but God was in the details.

The Holy Spirit wanted Tom to have a one–on–one intervention: one witness, me, with one Bible explaining the need for reconciliation with one God, through the only begotten Son, Christ Jesus our Lord. It worked marvelously because God was in the details. It took this type of crisis for Tom to be still and listen to the Holy Spirit; otherwise, dad would have never cried "Abba" but God was in the details.

Despite our frequently taking him out for the day, he longed for mountains, ocean views and the warm sunshine of Southern California. His ability to sustain independent living was gone. Dad's despondency led to psychological depression. I insisted on sessions of psychotherapy. In addition to psychotherapy, a weekly regiment of physical and occupational therapy was ordered. Nevertheless, dad, who never missed an opportunity to demonstrate stubbornness and obstinacy, refused to participate in physical therapy. As expected, eventually he became immobile. It became necessary to transport him via wheelchair. The dashing, handsome, independent gentleman was no longer able to walk. Making matters worse, he began experiencing Dysphagia. Dysphagia is a symptom of difficulty in swallowing. Dad was regularly transported to the hospital for cautionary measures due to this condition and repeated bouts with pneumonia. The fragility of life was obviously apparent. During Tom's last precautionary trip to the hospital x–rays revealed a tumor.

The biopsy confirmed my concerns. Dad had stage IV cancer. I spent considerable time with the oncological team. He was given only a few months.

Anthony and I decided to inform dad that a mass was found. But we choose not to disclose any specifics about cancer or subsequent treatment options. After numerous meetings with oncology, we decided against any surgical interventions. As a Palliative Care consultant, I knew what was about to happen next. After signing the ICF (Informed Consent Form), it was only a matter of time before a Hospice consultant arrived, my soul braced for impact – Glenn, son, here we go again.

Worshipping *Through* Fear

How many times did I visit Tom over the next few months? I don't know. I lost count. How many times did I walk on the very floor my mother transitioned from? I don't know that either. I do know that over the next two months, I sat in St. Elizabeth's hospital in liminality. I walked past myself in the corridor many times. Once, I may have even encouraged Glenn as we passed. He looked like he needed encouraging. As I looked out the window, a minivan was parking. Three children eagerly sprang out. The youngest ran towards the revolving door to visit Grandma Diane. I heard her mother say, "Ashley, stop running." I saw Chelly smiling and lovingly embracing each of those children as they entered the hospital lobby.

Mom's friend, Ms. Kay, she too was there ensuring that everyone had something nutritious to eat. I heard the voice of Dr. Ernest Perry, "Glenn we're going to take care of your mother." Images, voices, events of the past were now intersecting with my current day reality. I stepped away from the window as my tears flowed. The presence of the Holy Spirit helped me walk the corridor toward Dad's room. After conferring with the on-call doctor and assigned nurse, there was an intense need for me to pray for Tom. Upon completion of that prayer the heaviness lifted. My intercession for Tom was different that day. It felt like the last time I left mom's room – Déjà vu!

Heading back to Columbus was no easy task. Of course, my thoughts were continually on Tom. His health was failing. As expected, a few days later while standing in the kitchen, the Director of Nursing at the rehabilitative center called. She said, "Dr. Walter, your father's breathing is very shallow. And, please be advised that hospice is on premise." While hurriedly preparing to leave for Youngstown, a second call came, before I answered, I knew. Somehow, I just knew. "Dr. Walter your father has expired."

All the appropriate calls were made. Anthony met me after I arrived. We cried and prayed while collecting Dad's possessions. And of course, we made plans for the homegoing service.

Later that evening a spirit of fear came to harass me. It was intense. This haranguing lasted for days. Those old familiar snickering voices that visited me while standing in the unemployment line upon arriving in Columbus had returned. It has been my experience that most spiritual attacks occur during crisis, traumatic events or in route to achieving something great. Satan and those who love to practice wickedness have one common denominator, cowardliness. Cowards do not fight with any sense of honor. They do not present a frontal assault, ever. Our adversary is the chief architect of cowardliness. This spirit of fear came during my emotional vulnerability. Previously, these attacks lasted for only a moment. This time, however was very different. This attack lasted for days. It was relentless. Repeatedly, I heard failure in the spirit realm. Daily I fought the spiritual accusation of failure. "Your father died because of your poor decisions." It reverberated in my mind throughout days preceding the service.

As with Mom and Chelly, the Lord helped me write Dad's homegoing program. But Tony and I chose not to do a traditional service. We couldn't manage shaking the hands with a hundred people. Besides, very few people came to visit Tom during his illness. From our perspective their visits were not welcomed now. There was an incredible heaviness the morning of dad's funeral. I sat on a stool praying. Exhaustion prevented me from crying. While in route to the L.E. Blacks Funeral Chapel,

Bishop C. Shawn Tyson sent a message to me. It immediately strengthened me. L.E. Blacks did superior work but walking back into that building was excruciatingly painful! Memories of mom in a casket are indelibly etched in my memories. A multitude of thoughts flooded my mind walking toward the chapel. My niece, Tierra, greeted me at the chapel entrance. I embraced her, but my physical strength was depleted. I stood at the door unable to enter. My brother walked in and viewed dad's body. He purchased the burial suit. Like dad, Tony inherited an eye for finery. I could not look. I picked up my grandson and walked to the rear of the chapel instead of viewing the body.

The monster of fear was still fighting me. Jesus, please strengthen me for this task was my plea. "Are you crying grandpa?" My grandson asked. He touched my face with his precious little hand. God answered my prayer with His word: "Except you become as a child" softly rang in my spirit. I didn't have a comforting word for the family and guests until that moment. I was totally exhausted by the time the service started. The tears still flowed.

I took out my sunglasses and put them on. With all strength in me, I walked to the front of the room and stood parallel to the casket. I never looked at dad's body, I just couldn't. Fighting grief and emotionality my remarks were brief. In less than 10 minutes it was over.

I motioned for the undertaker to take charge of the service. Walking slowly toward the door, I spoke these words: "Lord I thank you for helping me today. I worship you." The spirit of fear immediately departed. Words are inadequate to express the relief I felt at that moment. It was instantaneously rapturous.

The interment was equally as brief. The various family members embraced and departed. I did not have the physical, emotional or spiritual strength to attend the dinner afterwards. It was over. Another chapter in the Walter family legacy was concluded. I drove past the area of Chelly's grave before leaving the cemetery. My mother's words came to mind. Mom took me shopping at Hills Department Store at Liberty Plaza on Belmont Avenue. I was 12 years old. It was a chilly Autumn Friday night. She bought an inexpensive gold digital watch for me. She excitedly sat down as we entered the house. She said exuberantly smiling, "Put the watch on and go show your father!" Tom was entertaining a friend. I walked into the room and showed him the watch. Never one to miss an opportunity to show off, Tom took one look and said, "I'm tired of you pimping off of me."

It didn't even bother me. I was already calcified. Nothing Tom did or said fazed me. Besides, I was ready to go to a community basement party. However, it devastated mom! She wept while sitting in the chair. I insisted that she stop. I said, "Mom, pay dad no attention. I am fine."

With a prophetic unction Diane said, "Glenn, hear me this night! Before Tom leaves this earth, he is going to need you, but you will not need him! Mark my words!" I think Diane would be pleased. Her son had learned how to worship through fear and live in reconciliation. In the words of psalmist John P. Key, "I've been *transformed*."

CHAPTER 2

WORSHIP

WHAT *is* WORSHIP?

What is worship? Worship is an act of submission that is accomplished in spirit and in truth. Worship requires an individual to surrender his will and wholly accept the will of our Lord and Savior Jesus Christ. Contrary to popular opinion, worship is not confined solely to an act of singing or dancing. Worship is not a tangible substance contained in religious paintings, ancient scrolls, or modern church hymnals. In fact, all human behavior in some capacity reflects worshipping. We were created with the need to worship.

God demonstrated the meaning of worship to me through a -beautiful experience one evening during the month of December. I was preparing to travel to Youngstown, Ohio, and join my family for a traditional New Year's Eve Watch Night church service. At the last-minute details were finalized, the presence of God filled the room. I was so moved by the Holy Spirit that tears began to fill my eyes. While sitting on the stairs and softly whispering the name of the Lord, the music by gospel recording artists, Commissioned ministered to my spirit. The song was entitled, "Learning to lean on you."

Without my understanding why, the Lord instructed me not to join my family in Youngstown. It took a while for me to accept that the Lord was instructing me to do the exact opposite of my will. Finally, with tears flowing down my face, my hands raised, my will broken, I was prepared to wholly accept the perfect will of God.

While sitting and meditating on the events of the evening, the Lord spoke to me: "This night you have worshipped me." The Lord revealed to me that the very essence of worship is when Christians truthfully relinquish their will and submit to His will. The Lord recognizes this process of submission as genuine worship.

That evening God explicitly instructed me to teach men and women how to worship Him. It is my sincere desire that you may be enlightened and encouraged by the worshipful experiences shared throughout this book. I have learned that Jesus will provide a worshipper with every means necessary to accomplish His divine purpose. God doesn't send us anywhere unless provisions are forthcoming to accommodate the assignment. He never drives you to accomplish a given task. Instead, as the Good Shepherd, He graciously leads us to a designated place for a specified period. For example, consider the Old Testament prophet Elijah (1 Kings 17:1-7 NASB):

Now Elijah the Tishbite, who was of the settlers of Gilead, said to Ahab, "As the Lord, the God of Israel lives, before whom I stand, surely there shall be neither dew nor rain these years, except by my word." The word of the Lord came to him, saying, "Go away from here and turn eastward, and hide yourself by the brook Cherith, which is east of the Jordan. It shall be that you will drink of the brook, and I have commanded the ravens to provide for you there." So he went and did according to the word of the Lord, for he went and lived by the brook Cherith, which is east of the Jordan. The ravens brought him bread and meat in the morning and bread and meat in the evening, and he would drink from the brook. It happened after a while that the brook dried up, because there was no rain in the land.

God leads us through valleys. He guides us through peril and all manner of treachery. But through it all, we learn to trust Him and depend on the promises of His Word. We learn how to worship Him in amid any occasion or event. May God give you understanding, heal all your spiritual wounds and increase your overall effectiveness as a New Testament worshipper. My friend, welcome to the next level of worship.

THE ACT of WORSHIPPING

The Bible does not systematically define worship. This book, however, will provide ecumenical information on worship. After reading and studying its contents, you'll better understand the true essence of worship.

The Scriptures do not mandate a designated form or style of worship. Jesus declared that anyone who desires to worship the Father must worship "in spirit and in truth" (St. John 4:24). A general survey of some terms and definitions refute the misconception that worship, and praise are always synonymous. In fact, worship could be narrowly regarded as the direct reverence or acknowledgment of God and His sovereignty, which require no specific act. More broadly, worship could be the direct acknowledgment of God and His divine supremacy, either by song, dance or sacrificial deeds; but especially by lifestyle (Rev. 4:9-11: to bow and do obeisance).

People pray to God because they desire to communicate their petitions. Often an individual praises God when he is cognizant of the things God has done (e.g., Exodus 15:1-21). But an individual can worship God regardless of what God does or does not perform. Prayer waits for an answer; worship does not require God to answer. Praise gives thanks; however, if God does not intervene in an affair, genuine worship would not be hindered.

To worship the Lord, an individual must be willing to forfeit personal agenda and acknowledge the absolute sovereignty of God and His divine plan for the individual's life.

When people truly worship God, they do not simultaneously make requests of God. We are by nature requestors constantly asking for something. God is by nature a giver. Therefore, when an individual worships God, he is not necessarily seeking spiritual answers nor requesting divine intervention, but, in fact, simply acknowledging the sovereignty of the Lord God Almighty through words, deeds, and a worshipful lifestyle.

THE WORSHIPPER

The most frequently used Greek word to render worship is (1) *proskuneo*. It means to make obeisance, do reverence to. It is most often used in regard to an act of homage or reverence to God (Vine, 1986). Consider: John 4:21-24; Revelation 5:14; 7:11; 11:16; 19:10; 22:9. (2) *latreuo* is another Greek word used to express reverence, awe or devotion to God in worship. Often the word was used to render religious service or homage (Vine, 1986). Consider: Philippians 3:3; Acts 7:42; Acts 24:14. An individual may raise his natural hands, dance with his natural feet, or shout with his natural voice but worship (3) *theosebes* is a spiritual function (Vine, 1986), (St. John 9:31).

Worshipping God in Spirit cannot be accomplished solely through fleshly presentations. Remember, genuine worship must be accomplished through Spirit and Truth.

(1) *proskuneo*: To make obeisance, occurs is St. John 4:23.

(2) *latreuo*: Devotion without request; to render service in Acts 24:14.

(3) *theosebes*: Reverencing God in St. John 9:31.

Chapter 3

WORSHIPPING

WORSHIPPING *in the* SPIRIT

Spirit (*pneuma*):

The trichotomy of a person is composed of body (*soma*), soul (*psyche*), and spirit *(pneuma)*. The elements composing the spiritual faculties of people are faith, hope, reverence, prayer and worship. This threefold spiritual composite must be wholly submitted to the Holy Spirit to biblically worship the Lord. The Greek word *pneuma* primarily denotes the wind, to breathe, blow. It especially refers to the spirit, but, like the wind, the spirit is invisible, immaterial and powerful.

There are several scriptures which help to describe and define the immaterial invisible part of people: Luke 8:55; Acts 7:59; I Corinthians 5:5; James 2:26; and Ecclesiastes 12:7. The spirit world is such an incredibly vast subject that the Holy Scriptures are full of the "supernatural" and spiritual occurrences. For that reason, the remainder of this chapter will be limited to concentrating on the spiritual nature of a person as it relates to worship.

The Apostle Paul identifies the Carnal in I Corinthians 3:1-3; the Natural in I Corinthians 2:14; and the Spiritual in I Corinthians 3:1; parts of a person.

The "Gates" to the *soma* (Body) are five senses: sight, smell, hearing, taste, and touch. The "gates" to the *psyche* (soul) are imagination, conscience, memory, reason, and affections. The gates of the *pneuma* (spirit) are faith, hope, reverence, prayer, and **WORSHIP**.

These gates permit corresponding communication between the senses. The gate of physical sight, our human "eyes" are the instruments by which the soul sees; it corresponds to the gate of the soul's imagination. The gate of hearing corresponds to the gate of the soul's memory, by which the soul recalls what it has heard.

The *pneuma* (spirit) does not have multiple gates. It has only one gate and it is an extremely powerful gatekeeper. Our spiritual sense faculties of faith, hope, reverence, prayer, and (most importantly) worship are constantly guarded by the powerful human will. The "will" gate must be opened before worship can be transacted. If your "will" gate remains stubbornly closed, genuine worship cannot take place. Worship will only take place when your "will" gate remains submissively open, which invites the Holy Spirit to interact with our Spiritual Person. Remember, God is not flesh and blood; He is a Spirit. Therefore, our relationship with Him is predicated upon spiritual interaction. That is why Jesus said: "They that worship me, must worship in spirit."

Regardless of how much the Natural Person attempts to understand the things of God, s/he simply cannot (I Corinthians 2:14). When Adam sinned, he spiritually disrupted the relationship between himself and God. Adam's sin "obstructed" God's access to the *pneuma* (spirit) of a person. What was once a divinely illuminated passage became a spiritually darkened storage area guarded by what the Bible calls a "stony heart," commonly known as the selfish human will.

The Bible often refers to the heart. Of course, it is not referring to the tissue of muscle that is responsible for circulating blood throughout the body. The spiritual heart is symbolic of the human will. Consider what God said in the book of Ezekiel 11:19-20:

"And I will give them one heart, and I will put a new spirit within you; and I will take the stony heart out of their flesh, and will give them a heart of flesh: that they may walk in my statutes, and keep them: and they shall be my people, and I will be their God."

Obviously, God is not going to physically perform heart surgery. Instead, He is going to spiritually remove a stony (hard) heart and replace it with a new (soft) heart of flesh. The word, "flesh," is symbolic to a substance that is soft and moldable. The Lord desires a will (heart) that is easily moldable and shapeable. The Potter must have soft clay to shape the vessel for His intended purpose.

Although people, composed of flesh and blood becomes weary, hungers for food, and requires rest, the Holy Spirit does not. The Spirit of the Lord is not susceptible to environments. It does not get cold nor does it hunger for food. The Holy Spirit empowers and enables all redeemed believers to overcome any environment and every circumstance (Acts 1:8; Philippians 4:13).

It is critically important to understand that our flesh is merely a costume for a spiritual being with an eternal soul. We must place emphasis on establishing and developing our spiritual relationship with the Lord. Of course, there will be occasions when we are not sure how we ought to pray. However, the Holy Spirit will help us and make intercession on our behalf (Romans 8:26). The Holy Spirit is consistent with the Word and Will of God because He is a manifestation of God.

The threefold nature of our personage must be wholly kept under subjection and sanctified by the Word of God (I Thessalonians 5:23; Hebrews 4:12). The flesh must be crucified to live in the Spirit, walk in the Spirit (Galatians 5:24-25), and most importantly, worship in the Spirit.

WORSHIPPING *in* TRUTH

Truth (*aletheia*):

The word "truth" has a multiplicity of meanings depending on who attempts to define its essence. A Roman politician once asked: "What is truth?" the Greek noun for truth, *aletheia*, signifies the reality lying at the basis of an appearance; it is the manifested veritable essence of a matter.

Perhaps truth is best defined by one who personifies its essence. Jesus gives the correct rendering of this word in all its fullness as embodied in Him. His statement in John 14:6 is subjective, yet totally accurate. God is ultimate truth. Therefore, the manifestations of God are also manifestations of truth. Truth is embodied in God's Son, exclaimed in God's Word, and revealed through God's Holy Spirit.

In the Old Testament, God required a High Priest to offer an atoning sacrifice for the sins of the entire nation of Israel. This sacred ritual required the offerer to be a moral practitioner of truth and God's holy commandments. The High Priest was required to complete several rituals before he could enter the Holiest of Holies where the Ark of the Covenant rested. The Ark was symbolic of God's presence.

The first phase took place in the outer court of the tabernacle. An offering was required to be placed upon the brazen altar.

The second phase required the High Priest to wash at a brazen laver. Phase three required the priest to make sacrificial offerings before entering the tabernacle. Once inside the tabernacle, he continued performing several rituals by lighting the lampstand of seven golden candlesticks, eating showbread from a specially crafted golden table, and lighting incense at a golden altar.

These preliminaries were essential for the High Priest to commune with God. Once a year the High Priest was required to pass through a veil and enter the Holiest of Holies to perform an atoning ritual for the sins of the entire nation. The Ark of the Covenant resided in the Holiest of Holies. For sins to be forgiven, a High Priest had to stand in the presence of the Ark sprinkling blood upon a preordained golden altar and offer an animal sacrifice. The sins of an entire nation were forgiven. If, however, one phase was inappropriately conducted, not one sin would be forgiven. This entire Old Testament offertory process was symbolic of what would be spiritually required for a New Testament born again worshipper.

Christ eliminated that Old Testament practice according to Hebrews 10:19-20. His sacrifice was sufficient for all humanity. We could not have access to eternal life without being spiritually covered by the blood of Jesus (Hebrews 9:1-28). And to worship the Lord, all veils of lying and hypocrisy must be removed (Hebrews 10:21-23).

Only an earnest heart will confess it is insufficient of itself and only a truthful person will admit he/she is greatly need of God's divine help. The entire Old Testament process of sacrificial offerings was only a prelude. Jesus personally provided the final sacrificial means by which sins could be forgiven! The only prerequisites for God's children to receive His forgiveness is to come, truthfully confessing and repenting of sins. The sinner, however, is required to repent and be spiritually reborn of water and spirit (Mark 16:16; Acts 2:38).

In the words of a gospel lyricist: you must "come to Jesus just as you are." These lyrics are not solely for the sinner. The truth of God's Word will compel men to confess their sins and faults in prayer. A sinner should not pretend to be sinless. Neither should Christians live in hypocrisy while simultaneously attempting to worship in truth. When cognizant of mistakes, admit them to God immediately, ask for forgiveness and do not continue to practice sinful activities (I John 3:1-9).

Be quick to forgive; be quick to repent. These Christian practices will make it possible to worship in truth. Remember, it is impossible to worship if you are not enveloped in truth. And you can't be in truth if you insist on living anti-scripturally. Embrace the truth and practice living truth, then, the truth will make you free. Because he whom the Son has set free, is free indeed (St. John 8:36).

Chapter 4

THE PURPOSE OF EXISTENCE

BORN AGAIN *to* WORSHIP

Why do we exist? What is our purpose for living? If we have a purpose, do we have a plan that will enable us to accomplish our purpose? The phrase "state of being" could be interpreted to mean: expression of explanation of existence. We were created in God's image. We are an expression of God's desire. We exist to glorify God through worship, praise and a lifestyle that compels others to follow our example (I Corinthians 11:1). King Solomon wrote: "Fear God and keep his commandments: for this is the whole purpose of man" (Ecclesiastes 12:13). To discover our purpose, we must seek Him that created us and live according to His instructions. A synoptic comparison of the first three Gospels reveal the principles of the Kingdom of God as they relate to the purpose of our existence. Jesus Christ reveals those principles through preaching and teaching. He provided humanity with instructions on how to obtain eternal life with Him (St. Matthew 6:19-34 & St. John 3:5-15).

Worshipping the Lord is a means of expressing the soul's ultimate desire. Remember, worship always requires a surrendered will. A surrendered will is achieved through prayer and fasting.

As we pray and fast our will is spiritually sacrificed. The Bible explains the process: "He must increase, but I must decrease (St. John 3.30)." Adamic carnality relentlessly drives us toward pleasing ourselves. The Holy Spirit gently leads us toward pleasing God and thereby helping others to know of God and His goodness (St. Matthew 5:14-16).

As sanctified born-again worshippers, we must always be mindful that we serve an omniscient God. Our conduct and behavior should reflect the fact that we are always in God's presence. The Holy Ghost is the unseen guest at our local church dinner, a listener who is privy to our every conversation, and the guest evangelist living in our homes. As Christians we choose to live holy because holiness pleases our Lord (I Peter 1:15-16). Christian worshippers do not practice sinning because sinful activity displeases and dishonors our Lord and Savior Jesus Christ. Christians must live holy to preserve the mind of Christ (Philippians 2:5). Remember, you were born again to worship.

The Bible instructs people everywhere to pray and pray without ceasing (II Timothy 2:8; I Thessalonians 5:17). These verses provide insight to God's expectations regarding the prayer life of born-again worshippers. God expects us to have a prayerful mentality and be willing to pray whenever needed. Praying must become as much a part of our daily agenda as communicating and socializing. It would be impossible to live a natural fulfilling life if we were completely unable to communicate and socially interface with others.

It is also impossible to live a spiritually fulfilling life without being able to communicate with God through prayer and experiencing His divine blessings. Therefore, for Christians, prayer is not optional, but in fact, a critical part of our daily lives. The combination of prayer and worship keeps the spiritual salt of the earth fresh. If the salt loses its savor, it is good for nothing, "but to cast out and trodden under foot of men" (St. Matthew 5:13). The Word of God instructs us to live holy as an example to unholy people. The kingdom of darkness will not be conquered by Christians who are easily intimidated. It will take bold prayerful Holy Ghost-filled Christians who are dedicated worshippers! Worshipping in the spirit is the beginning of a life-long love affair with Christ. It is through this process of submission and surrender that our hearts open to God's irreplaceable love.

Chapter 5

WORSHIPPING THROUGH CALAMITY

JOB: THE UPRIGHT SERVANT of GOD

In the Old Testament, the Books of Job, Psalms, Proverbs, Ecclesiastes, and Song of Solomon are considered works of literary art. Academically, the book of Job is a beautiful work of ancient poetic literature. The literary structure and quality of oratory skills are incredibly brilliant. The centrality of this book serves as a profound statement regarding the subject of theodicy (God's justice in light of human suffering).

Is God nearby when we are confronted with tragedy? Is God aware of our loved ones lying unconscious in the Intensive Care Unit? Was God present when the news of death finally reached your ear? Did God feel your grief and sadness at the funeral? If Job were alive, he would volunteer to take the witness stand and emphatically answer yes to all the above questions!

The book of Job provides us with the profile of an Old Testament patriarch who knew how to worship through the unexplainable. The writer probably had access to written sources that, under divine inspiration, defined the character and nobility of Job:

"There was a man in the land of Uz, whose name was Job; and that man was perfect, upright, and one that feared God, and eschewed evil" (Job 1:1). Job's willingness to acknowledge the sovereignty of God in every circumstance, even the most tragic, serves as an academic case study of pure genuine worship.

The writer meticulously details the specific events of the day when Job's sons and daughters gathered together at the eldest brother's house to eat and drink. While his children were eating and drinking a messenger came to Job with the message that the Sabeans had stolen all his oxen and mules and had killed his servants with swords. A second messenger entered Job's house while the first messenger was yet speaking. The second messenger informed Job that a fiery storm had completely consumed his sheep.

The third messenger entered the house while the second was yet speaking. He reported that the Chaldeans had stolen the camels and killed the servant with swords. Before the third messenger concluded his report a fourth and final messenger entered. He informed Job that while his children were eating and drinking a great wind storm arose and destroyed his eldest son's house and none of his children survived.

It is utterly impossible to define or even attempt to describe Job's emotional state of being. I can only surmise that this man was devastated. Nevertheless, he arose from sitting, shaved his head (a customary cultural ritual of humiliation) and fell upon the ground and worshipped! Consider his statement:

> "Naked came I out of my mother's womb, and naked shall
> I return thither: the Lord gave, and the Lord hath taken away;
> blessed be the name of the Lord"
>
> ~ Job 1:21

Dear born-again believer, please understand Job's words. His words did not comprise a prayer because he was not making requests. Job did not offer God verbal praise because he was not grateful or thankful for the death of his children. But, in one statement Job did acknowledge the absolute sovereignty of the LORD (Elohim/Creator), even in tragedy.

Job never asked God: Why didn't you intervene? Or, how could you have allowed this terrible thing if you really cared about me? In this life we will often have experiences that are devastating. During these times we might be tempted to blame God for the things that cannot be easily explained. We might intellectualize that God is punishing us as a consequence of our actions or inactions.

There will be times when we'll ask the Lord: Why? We must understand, as the prophet Daniel did, we are greatly loved despite events or circumstances (Daniel 10:11). The Holy Spirit will help us to understand that tragedy is not necessarily God's punishment. Remember, the Lord God blessed the latter end of Job's life more than the beginning (Job 42:12).

The Bible states that during all of Job's troubles he did not charge God foolishly (Job 1:22). It is impossible to measure the hurt, pain, and suffering of someone in Job's circumstance. How can anyone adequately prepare for the shock of a tragedy? Tragedy usually forces people to hide behind the defense mechanism of denial. It causes tremendous suffering, grief, pain, and often leaves us speechless.

Tragedy has another property not often discussed. It has the inexplicable ability to make the crooked straight. People who are avowed enemies will work together during and after a disastrous tragedy. Family members, who have not spoken to each other for years, will embrace and forgive each other after an unexplainable tragedy.

Chapter 6

WORSHIPPING THROUGH TRANSFORMATION

DAVID: THE SERVANT *After*
GOD'S OWN HEART

Have you ever considered the various stages of transition for a caterpillar to become a butterfly? The scientific term used to define this process of change is called "metamorphosis." Simply put, metamorphosis is a process of transformation or of changing forms. Who decided that the caterpillar should not always crawl upon the earth but fly above it? God did. The Lord created the creatures that both crawl and fly. The caterpillar is unique because it has a perspective on both crawling and flying. As a child my daughter, Ashley Nicole, did not like ugly furry crawling bugs, but she loved beautiful bright multi–colored butterflies. I had to teach her that God made everything beautiful in His own time! (Ecclesiastes 3:11).

The Lord uses the process of transition to transform or change us in due season! (Ecclesiastes 3:1-8). Unfortunately, many people, even some Christians, really believe in transition but not change. How can that be possible? Our Government has spent billions of dollars relocating people to better houses in respectable communities. But, if the inward nature of the people has not been changed, the purpose of the move is in vain.

I assure you, the new neighborhood will soon resemble the old neighborhood. Yes, they were moved, but they were not changed. How would you describe a person who frequently attempts to romance someone's husband or wife? Apparently, their old night club habits have not changed. Yes, they've moved from the bar stool to the church pew, but their behavior has not changed!

To be a son or daughter of God, we must go through transition (Acts 2:38). We must be spiritually transformed or changed by the renewing of our minds (Romans 12:2). After we have gone through transition, we are then transformed or changed, and capable of overcoming the systems of this world (I John 5:4).

The son of Jesse, David, did not exactly look like an ugly bug, David had handsome features and a ruddy complexion (I Samuel 16:13). But there was something exceptional about David, other than his physical features. This exceptional quality could not be seen with the natural eye. God, however, saw the moldable will of David and He liked it (I Samuel 16:7). The Lord knew David would make mistakes; nevertheless, He saw David after transformation, in his butterfly form.

The Lord let David know that one day he would become Saul's successor. God gave David a preview of that event, albeit it did not change the events that would precede the transitional phase to David's kingship. Perhaps the caterpillar knows the dangers of having to crawl across busy intersections and make its cocoon in trees where birds dwell.

Nevertheless, pain and danger are part of the transition. The caterpillar knows that one day car wheels will no longer be a threat to its existence! As David grew in wisdom and strength, his popularity and influence also grew. King Saul became jealous of David and attempted to kill him. David had to leave the city and live in caves, but it was just another phase of the Lord's transition plan. Soon after Saul's death David was anointed King!

Kings often make mistakes and David was no exception. He had an adulterous affair with a woman named Bathsheba and she became pregnant. David arranged to have Bathsheba's husband Uriah killed in combat. The Lord was greatly displeased with David (II Samuel 11) and allowed the new-born child to become very sick. David began to fast and pray for his child (II Samuel 12:16).

How tragic! The great king was losing his child. As David lay upon the earth, fasting and praying, he wept because of his sinful actions. He had destroyed a marriage and murdered someone's husband. The mighty king had brought a reproach upon himself and the kingdom. On the seventh day of the fast, David saw his servants whispering. Immediately, he knew the child had died.

David arose. He not only arose physically, but he arose spiritually. David was not the same man who had lain on the earth, wallowing in shame and sorrow.

The Bible says: David arose from the earth, and washed, and anointed himself, and changed his apparel, and came into the house of the Lord, and worshipped: then he came to his own house; and when he required, they set bread before him, and he did eat (II Samuel 12:20). David rolled in dirt like a peasant for seven days, burdened by his sinful deeds. But when he got up, he washed and anointed himself. Then he worshipped! His will was broken, his mind transformed. David had emptied himself of lust and deceit. He wanted only the will of God!

Chapter 7

WELCOME TO THE NEXT LEVEL

ACCEPTING *the* CALL

Worship is the key to activating God's blessings and learning how to live in the realm of the miraculous. Worship is the key to experiencing Kingdom living. In the early eighties there was a popular song entitled: "Name it, claim it." God used the lyrics of that song to reveal the importance of being specific in prayer. Unfortunately, many people misunderstood the message in the song. They didn't realize that lifestyle was a factor in "claiming" God's blessings. Yes, we can name it, but if our lifestyle is not pleasing to God, we aren't claiming anything.

As we grow in wisdom, it becomes easier to discern the difference between human ideas and the mind of God. The Holy Spirit leads, but human selfishness always drives. The Holy Spirit prays through us for the perfect will of God to be manifested in our lives. Human nature seeks its own satisfaction.

Only a self-indulgent person really believes everything claimed by faith must come to fruition. We can pour imported olive oil on every sidewalk in America, but if our lifestyle is not ordained by God, how can we claim by faith what God never intended for us to possess? Ask the Lord to reveal to you His divine purpose for your life and, when He does, accept it without question!

Early in my ministry, I felt the Lord leading me to leave Dayton, Ohio and move my family to Detroit, Michigan in preparation for the pastorate. After weeks of entertaining the spirit of fear, I decided it was not a good idea to go. What a devastating mistake! Essentially, my actions told God that I know what is best for me. The results of my disobedience nearly destroyed my family and ruined my life.

Seven years later the Lord spoke to me while in prayer. He instructed me to feed His sheep. Although, He did not indicate a specific city as yet, it was clear the Lord had extended His favor to me again. What an honor and privilege to serve a God of second chances. Early on September morning, while in route to Youngstown, Ohio, the Lord spoke three words to me while approaching Columbus: "Behold the city." At that moment the presence of God simply overwhelmed me.

It was difficult explaining to people how the Lord used three words to provide instructions. In retrospect, it was unwise to expect some people to understand, especially those who couldn't identify faith if it were sold in bright orange bottles at the local grocery store. There is always a risk in sharing too much information prematurely (Proverbs 29:11). Often, we want to share some portion of our revelation with a family member, friend or business associate. Our enthusiasm to share may not be met with the same level of adulation.

Perhaps, it is best that we keep the doors of our mouth shut until the Holy Spirit gives us permission to speak. Unfortunately, for many of us that is extremely hard to do. Nevertheless, with God all things are possible to them that believe and to them that learn to keep quiet!

PURSUING *the* CALL

One evening the same hideous spirit of fear that hindered me earlier in my life returned. The presence of fear was literally suffocating that night. My mind was flooded with potential failures. I heard evil voices sarcastically saying: "You're going to fail, the Lord never told you to go to Columbus."

This was unprecedented in my life. A frightful experience was about to happen. While walking and praying, fear intensified until breathing was difficult. The confrontation became physical. The assault was emotionally draining. I was unable to speak words.

Exhausted, I lay on the kitchen floor, weeping like a child. The Holy Spirit asked me a question: "What is your name?" I answered, "Lord, you know my name." "What is it?" He asked. "My name is Glenn. I'm scared because I don't want to fail again." Instantly, the spirit of fear departed. The Lord informed me that Glenn never allowed himself to heal; therefore, this experience was necessary.

The Lord spoke healing to my spirit and ministered to my very troubled mind. Jesus empowered me to proceed and succeed from the memory of failure!

The first time Peter attempted to trust Jesus was by walking on water. He failed (St. Matthew 14:28). Jesus had to extend His hand to Peter and rescue him. But, after Peter was empowered with the Holy Ghost, the Apostle extended his hand to a crippled man and said: "Silver and gold have I none; but such as I have give I thee: In the name of Jesus Christ of Nazareth rise up and walk." The first time Jesus had to extend his hand to help Peter. However, after Peter was empowered, he was able to extend his hand to help others. Peter succeeded from the memory of failure (Acts 3:1-11). Although, every detail was meticulously planned, Jesus rearranged my agenda. In retrospect, God did me a favor, by allowing me to have that experience. If I would have moved to Columbus without being changed, failure was inevitable. My change came in the form of being able to forgive myself and accept God's complete healing.

Our ministry in Dayton was ending. Friends who had invested in our ministry with their prayers, words of encouragement, and financial gifts did not want us to leave, but they understood. Many faithful people came to assist us with cleaning and packing. I watched an Elder scrub our living room floor on his hands and knees. One family invited us to stay with them for several days, until our furniture was delivered to Columbus.

This same family had just given my wife and me several hundred dollars to help defray moving costs. May the blessings of the Lord be upon them forever. Of course, there were those precious darlings whose weekly canned sermon included the following warning to me: "Beware the train that leaves before its time." I know God has a blessing for them as well.

PROVISIONS *with* THE PROMISE

We had given up four bedrooms and a two-car garage for a split-level town house and no garage. Nevertheless, we were residents of Ohio's Capital. It was an extremely small price to pay for being in the center of God's will. After several days of unpacking, it was time to telephone my future employer. I was excited about my new career as an Education Consultant for the State of Ohio.

The Governor, however, was apparently not as excited. He delayed signing the lease and approving the funds for the new building that contained my office. It was not politically convenient to expend tax dollars on buildings during an election year. After several weeks of waiting, it became obvious that politics were a major factor in the lives of every state employee. This was an unexpected challenge for me but not God. It was time to market my skills to other potential employers. During the following weeks of unsuccessful job searching we felt isolated and lonely, but the Lord was with us.

Perhaps a young shepherd boy named David could empathize with us. An individual could get very lonely sitting on mountain slopes watching sheep graze. After receiving several "Sorry, but you're over-qualified" letters, a friend suggested filing for unemployment benefits. My wife insisted on coming and bringing all three children. It was her way of saying they would always love me without reservation.

While standing in the unemployment line with my $500.00 eel skin briefcase, those old familiar voices began whispering: "You're going to fail, the Lord never told you to go to Columbus." After applying for unemployment assistance, that old sense of failure returned. My companion tried to encourage me but to no avail. We sat in the van and watched our children play in the parking lot. Although, I did not want the family to see me crying, my face reflected agony accompanied with many tears.

One morning, while I was in prayer, the Lord spoke to me and said: "Stop asking me for a job. Praise me; I've already prepared a job for you!" The next 30 days were difficult, but only in my mind. Being unemployed was unchartered water for me. Oh, I knew joy was coming in the morning, but the Lord had to teach me how to worship through the night (Psalm 30:5). We were learning how to practice "believing to see" the goodness of the Lord in the land of the living (Psalm 27:13). Often, Christians quote that scripture whenever challenges, especially unexpected challenges manifest themselves.

Although, we were in a county with over a million people, there was an incredible sense of loneliness and isolation. But God revealed to me that great visions and divine revelations do not come to massive crowds. There are times when God insists on being alone with us. The Bible, especially throughout the Old Testament economy, is replete with examples of great people that were isolated prior to being elevated to the purpose of God.

Consider: Elijah was alone on the mountain when he heard the still small voice of God (I Kings 19:11-13); Joshua was alone when he bowed before the captain of the Lord's host (Joshua 5:14-15); Moses was alone on the mountain when God commissioned him to liberate Israel (Exodus 3:6-10); Daniel was alone when he saw the vision of God (Daniel 10:7-12); Isaiah was alone when he beheld God's glorious train filling the temple (Isaiah 6:18); Peter was alone praying on the housetop when Jesus opened his understanding (Acts 1:9-16); and John was imprisoned and isolated on Patmos when he wrote the Revelation of Jesus Christ (Revelation 1:9).

During the next thirty days I found help in the person of pastor, Dr. Eugene Lundy. His God-inspired counsel and guidance were paramount in helping us during this difficult time. He and Dr. Kay Lundy were empathetic. Although, Pastor and Sister Kay Lundy held doctorate degrees, they never offered rehashed theological textbook rhetoric.

Instead, they demonstrated kindness. Pastor reassured me: "God will honor your obedience and meet every need, just stay on your sanctified bony knee caps." Several days after he made that statement I was offered a position as Office Manager by the Director of Franklin County Adult Probation Services. The possibilities of growth in this job were endless, and so were the politics. My responsibilities included preparing docket information for eighteen Common Pleas Court judges and supervising nineteen administrative support staff personnel.

The Lord was with me and within six months my salary increased by nearly $2,000.00. Soon, I was overseeing nineteen employees matrixed throughout three departments: Customer Service, Intake Services, and the Records Department.

I was fully prepared for the demands of leadership, having been trained in the latest management philosophies. However, I was totally unprepared for jealous folk who hate the success of others. My head often ached while driving home. Have you ever wondered why being successful provokes jealously in some of your peers? The Probations Department had an incredible employee turnover during my tenure. However, of my nineteen employees only one departed, due to being offered a $6,000.00 increase. Three of my staff members were awarded the Franklin County's Employee of the Quarter Performance Award.

It became quite evident that God was using this political environment only to spiritually educate me. Although, my soul yearned to go and work in the private sector, the Lord kept convincing me to stay. One day a staff member came into my office and said: "Glenn, I don't claim to be a religious person, but last night the Lord told me to come in here and tell you to stay right here." She pointed her finger at me, turned and walked out. My first inclination was to remove my name plate and insert a sign reading: Welcome to Balaam's office. Enter at your own risk! (Numbers 22:18-34).

I certainly needed to reevaluate my goals and priorities. After all, my spiritual orders did not read: Go forth and climb the corporate ladder. Besides, promotion and power come from nowhere on earth, but from God (Psalm 75:6 TLB). The Lord's agenda for me was clear: Stop seeking other employment; serve in this position as a Christian ambassador; be an excellent example and learn how to worship in any environment. The Lord taught me how to ignore jealousy and yet love jealous people. He taught me how to befriend and love Judas, but, whenever absent, always place John the Beloved in charge!

One beautiful August morning while I was driving to work, the Lord spoke to me: "It's over; praise me." I thought the Lord was about to remove some office pharaohs who were requiring my staff to make bricks without straw. The praises of God flowed from my mouth all day long!

During September, however, the meaning of "It's over" became quite apparent. My professional tenure of fifteen months with the County was ending.

A dear sister in Christ called me from Children's Services to ascertain some court information regarding one of her cases. During the conversation she made a statement that profoundly impacted me. "When I saw you yesterday, you appeared to be out of place." She continued, "It's as if you no longer belong there." My intellect rejected the comment, but my spirit received every prophetic word she spoke. Things began to happen that were irrefutably the hand of God. Just as the Lord opened doors that people could not shut, now God was closing doors that people could not open.

Any doubt that lingered was removed from my mind when the Holy Spirit sent a person whom I hired to ask me: "Do you know what season you're in?" I thought silently, my season? She obviously discerned uncertainty in my facial expression. "Yes, your time" she said. "It must be your time in the Kingdom." There could be no mistaking the collaborative efforts of the Holy Spirit. The Lord was deliberate and His agenda for me was distinctively clear. It was time to resign and proceed without caution to the next level.

I would be untruthful if I stated that I had everything figured out. There were many things that remained quite nebulous. I really did not have a solidified plan for the immediate future. Nope, I didn't know what I was going to do the next week, for that matter, the next day was equally as uncertain. This was a step of faith. Well, this was a gigantic leap of faith. This leap of faith was equivalent to Evil Knievel jumping across the Snake River Canyon in a flaming rocket without a parachute!

My father once said, "Son, hindsight is 20/20." Of course, that means after an event has occurred, it is easy to determine the correctness or meaningfulness of that decision. It was my most sincere conviction that this specific position was ending. There were many factors too numerous to explain. Suffice it to say, I believed that the Lord was with me in this decision. Could I have waited until securing another job? Yes, in retrospect, probably. Nevertheless, my attitude was to hoist the flag; tomorrow, we sail!

Although, my family did not completely understand my resignation, they accepted it. After notifying them, it was time to inform the department of my decision. As expected, many were disappointed, and others were too busy with their own lives to even be concerned. The next forty days of my prayer life were incredible. Instead of moaning and complaining to God about not immediately revealing His long-term plan to me, every morning I offered the Lord sincere praise and Thanksgiving (Psalm 71:8). With each day, the praise became more affectionate, more passionate. Only after praising God would family needs be mentioned in prayer.

The will of God was paramount to me. All the cruel jealous stunts performed by previous coworkers were insignificant. There was freedom and healing in the praise! Are you hurting from past experiences and in desperate need of healing? Then praise God! Problems seemed to miraculously subside; our financial situation seemed less critical. This was pure unrehearsed praise. My spirit was in perfect harmony with the will of God. And this perfect spiritual alignment was the quintessence of worship: to relinquish my will and submit to the will of the Heavenly Father. In retrospect, praising God was building a spiritual platform for the Holy Spirit to fill our home with His presence.

Remember, the Holy Spirit is not rude. He will not enter where He is not wanted! We must invite Him to come into the midst of our circumstances. Praising God rolls out the spiritual red carpet and declares: Lord, please come by here! It was during this time that God confirmed His Word to me. Although, we had absolutely no money, each day we ate. Our cupboards remained full. We did not have to ask our neighbors for a single slice of bread or a cup of sugar. We paid our utilities. People who were not aware of our circumstance bestowed financial blessings upon us. One woman wrote a check for $600.00 and asked if it was enough.

I discovered a new realm of praise in Christ. This dimension was marvelous indeed! It far exceeded the ritual of repeating old stale canned prayers. Each day began with a glorious and spiritually fresh praise service. The incredible presence of the Almighty God was sweeping through our home in such a resplendent magnificent way, it was wonderful and miraculous!

This was the voice-activated realm! Each day we watched God masterfully provide everything from nothing but our faith. Only the element of time precluded our prayers from being answered. Whatever we prayed for, there was no doubt – the blessing was on the way. Things were happening exactly like the Word of God said. Whatsoever you loose on earth He will loose in Heaven (St. Matthew 18:18). Why did it take so long for me to arrive in this realm?

Perhaps it was time to blindly trust God without reservation and learn the meaning of walking by faith and not by sight (II Corinthians 5:7). It was time to trust God with no source of income, no prospect of employment, no government subsistence, no Blue Cross or Blue Shield, just faith in Jesus who died on the cross. The spiritual intelligentsia would call my decision blatant reckless disregard for the family's overall holistic well-being. The conservative right would call my decision a poor moral judgment! The theological scholar would call my decision an immensely inaccurate hermeneutical application of an exegesis. But, the Bible calls it agreeing with the will of God. The first time we were without income was terrifying, even with unemployment benefits. The second time we learned that God is not a man that He should lie (Numbers 23:19). At last, I'd found the secret place of which King David spoke (Psalm 91).

It was no longer necessary for me to stand on the spiritual river banks "fishing" for a blessing. In this voice-activated realm, fish come to the fisher, you simply must learn how to lower your net down on the "right side" and command the fish to swim into it (St. John 21:3-6). There are no "just can't do it folk" in this realm. Ashley Nicole often complained about not being able to ride her bike as fast as her friends.

She convinced me to remove her training wheels. After falling many times, she said "Daddy, I just can't do it." I directed her attention toward her brothers. Almar and Phillip were speeding past the house as if racing in the Tour de France. The next day Ashley was riding without falling. She concretely decided: It was time for the next level! Are you ready for the next level?

The Lord was teaching me how to successfully operate in the Kingdom instead of merely functioning in the church. The spiritual lessons learned during that 40-day transition period are still vividly memorable. On one occasion, while praying about some short-term needs, the Lord gave me assurance of long-term success. The Lord said that there were "great things planned for my life, things that I knew not of." Although, I was praying in a public area, blessing God out loud was completely in order! Why? Despite that immediate concern voiced in my prayer the Lord had just indirectly responded to every unspoken concern in my heart. He said: "things were planned…" And, for me to partake of whatever God had planned, He would have to bring me through the present situation. The joy of the Lord filled my soul in that instant. Is there really any wonder that God testified and said: "To whom then will you liken me, or shall I be equal (Isaiah 41:25)?" Simply put, Lord, there is nobody else like you and no God beside you (Isaiah 44:8).

Are you ready for the next level? If the answer is yes, then allow me the privilege of extending an invitation to you. Come join millions of worshippers who already live in the realm of the miraculous and understand the biblical principles of a spiritual voice-activated Kingdom. Beloved, discern your call and pursue it. Remember, pursue the promise and God will make provisions. The Lord provided me with another job, working for a National Christian Retailing Company. Take my advice and get ready for the next level!

Chapter 8

WORSHIPPING IN WARFARE

THE *Crazy* PRAISE

Crazy is a word used to describe the behavior of an individual who has lost contact with the reality of their immediate environment. I am convinced that no other word more accurately and adequately describes the behavior of a worshipper, who has learned how to lose contact with the circumstances of their environment and worship God despite of what is happening or has previously happened.

Spiritual battlefields are often cluttered with spiritually wounded trainees who never attended biblical training sessions. Perhaps these trainees felt superior and sincerely believed they required no further spiritual combat preparation. They later discovered, however, that they were sincerely wrong.

Some new recruits never learned how to effectively gird their loins with truth, put on a breastplate of righteousness, don a helmet of salvation, protect themselves with a shield of faith, or, most importantly, destroy the enemy with the sword of the Spirit. Wherefore, put on the whole armor of God that you may be able to stand against the devil (Ephesians 4:11-17).

After you have completed spiritual basic training you will move to soldier status and learn how to endure hardness (persevere and overcome) as a good soldier of Jesus Christ. Learning how to endure hardness is a definite sign of maturity in the born-again worshipper (II Timothy 2:3-4). Every Christian must strive to attain the next level. Eventually we will reach a level that enables us to worship God in the midst of intense spiritual combat.

It is not logical to worship God when we're in an undesirable situation or environment. Human logic will suggest that we not worship God until everything in our life is pleasingly perfect. However, true biblical worship is not logical, nor can it be explained by relying on philosophical human concepts, such as deductive reasoning. Logic only permits conceivability. Worship elevates us above human understanding and perfectly aligns our mind with the mind of Christ. Having a God-centered mind will keep us in perfect peace, even in a hostile environment (Isaiah 26:3-4). All things are possible with the mind of Christ (Philippians 4:13). Even a squared circle becomes a possible reality in the mind of a Spirit-filled worshipper (Mark 9:23). Receive that.

God empowered Joseph with the gift of interpreting dreams. Joseph endured many hardships, but he never stopped utilizing his gift. It would have been easy for Joseph to sit in an Egyptian prison and bitterly complain about the great injustice of being accused of attempting to rape a military officer's wife (Genesis 39:1-20). However, Joseph, like his father, was a worshipper, and Brother Joseph had obviously learned how to worship while in warfare.

Joseph had become a seasoned spiritual soldier tempered with patience. He was not easily provoked or distressed. He had learned how to love family members and neighbors who were envious and jealous of his God-given gifts. Joseph knew how to work next to jealous folk who lay awake at night scheming and planning his demise. He was able to worship God even after being thrown into a pit that was prepared for him by his own brothers. Joseph worshipped the Lord while being transported to Egypt by merchants. He worshipped Jehovah while standing on an Egyptian auction block – about to be sold as human merchandise.

Joseph was able to maintain a Godly disposition even while serving in prison for a crime he never committed. You see, Joseph had learned the secret of the crazy praise! There was no doubt in his mind that, even though he was serving time in prison, a change was soon to take place! (Genesis 39:21-23).

The plan of God is so masterful! The Genesis writer must have felt exuberance as the Almighty God revealed to him the details of Joseph's life. Studying Joseph's life is comparable to watching the sunrise on the banks of the Yellow Sea. Imagine for a moment that you are standing on the southern coastline of Korea looking across a vast measureless sea. There appears to be a small seemingly insignificant object rising from the water, and as it begins to ascend, the clouds leisurely begin to glow.

Slowly, the reddish orange clouds dissipate as if they were announcing that God has saved the best for last! A brief pause occurs and then the tip of what appears to be a slightly glowing oval-shaped object finally pierces the horizon. Hardly anyone seems to notice, yet with each passing moment, the object becomes larger, brighter while refracting its glistening awesomeness of the atmosphere.

When the appropriate time comes, however, everyone will realize that this is not a dull oval-shaped object. The object appears to be round, and it isn't dull; it is astonishingly bright! The higher it rises the more it dominates the entire sky, until the very sea that briefly seemed to contain it, now reflects its majestic brilliance. Finally, when this mammoth star, known as the sun has climbed to its zenith, everyone in the eastern hemisphere will recognize its greatness!

Beloved, receive a word from the Lord this very moment. You're a spiritual Joseph on the rise, and when you can't say when, or how, or why, simply say yes. Learn how to throw your hands up and give God some praise. A crazy praise! Soon everyone around you will recognize your greatness in God. Selah! The crazy praise will usually precede total surrender. Total surrender will usher you into the realm of genuine worship. That's why it is paramount that you stop trying to understand everything that happens in your life. The will of God is not a multi-colored cube toy for you to manipulate. God's will is perfect. Besides, your footsteps have already been ordered and ordained by God (Psalm 37:23). You need only to surrender to the perfect leading of the Holy Spirit. Stop fretting about past mistakes and learn how to succeed from the memories of failure.

Perhaps Joseph's life could have been less complicated had he not informed his brothers of the dreams. Maybe there were times when Joseph's zeal slightly surpassed his wisdom. The Lord instructed the Genesis writer to record Joseph's unwise choices as an example to us. Albeit, God's masterful plan always leaves room for His servants to recover and heal. Remember King David's prayer: "O spare me until I recover strength, before I go hence and be no more" (Psalm 39:13).

You will experience some difficulties as you begin your spiritual ascension to the next level of Christian maturity. Nevertheless, your difficulties will help you learn how to endure hardness as a good soldier. Your desire to please Jesus will inevitably increase your commitment to serve in God's Kingdom. The more you commit, the higher you ascend. The higher you ascend in Christ, the more you reflect the Son's glory.

Recently, I was in Dallas, Texas, on business. I changed flights in Atlanta, Georgia. As the airplane approached Atlanta, the captain informed us that the control tower ordered him to abort the landing and initiate holding pattern procedures. As rain began to fall, the pilot informed us that we were climbing to a higher altitude while awaiting further instructions. Suddenly the lights inside the cabin began to blink and the air conditioner ceased to work. Seemingly, the longer we waited for the control tower to provide instruction, our situation became increasingly worse. After landing and docking, the pilot apologized and informed us that the plane was caught in some cross winds. Unfortunately, the winds were unavoidable.

Perhaps God has you in a holding pattern. It is not quite time for you to reach your destination. Therefore, until you receive directions from the heavenly control tower, you must wait for further instructions. It is very possible that you might incur some temporary turbulence from the cross winds of jealousy and envy, but be patient and learn how to endure hardness while you wait.

Like Moses, we must learn how to stand still, even when Pharaoh's chariots are charging directly toward us. We must learn the power of the crazy praise. Remember those two ministers who were beaten and imprisoned, yet at midnight they sang songs and offered praises unto God (Acts 16:25). Brothers and sisters, I want you to know those were crazy praises!

On a brisk autumn afternoon, one of my family members was in an automobile accident. Another member was transported directly to the emergency room; a different member was seen in the emergency room for chest pains; and yet, another was seen for heart complications. Early about 2:30 a.m., while walking the fourth floor of the hospital, it occurred to me that some people would not have withstood the mental pressure. Realizing my need to pray, the Lord helped me to find an empty waiting room. I began to pray. While in prayer, the Holy Spirit revealed to me that the devil had been given permission to "box" against me, but he had failed to produce the "knockout punch" and the Lord had just rung the bell to officially end the match.

Upon receiving that revelation, it was necessary for me to ignore Glenn's mind and allow the perfect mind of Christ to operate in me (Philippians 2:5). While walking down the corridor back to mother's room with my arms raised in victory, my mouth spoke His praise. Yes, the crazy praise!

We cannot negotiate with the enemy of our soul. Can you imagine Moses trying to negotiate with Pharaoh's charging chariot? Stop trying to manipulate the will of God. Accept the fact that you are where God wants you for a reason, even if cross winds are fiercely blowing. Just be assured in Christ that blowing winds only last for a season. We are soldiers on temporary assignment.

The Lord often uses temporary experiences to accomplish long-term results in our lives (II Corinthians 4:17). Consider yourself blessed. God is doing you a favor by allowing you to experience this season. Soon you will be a dynamic worshipper, fully prepared to accept the mission that once seemed impossible! Therefore, let's quickly dispose of selfishness, for we must decrease, but he must increase (St. John 3:30). Very soon, it'll not only be your season, it will be your turn!

God will often place a worshipper amid chaos. This gives us an opportunity to triumphantly reflect the brightness of the Son. Also, it empowers us to become His witnesses. Therefore, let your radiant light shine before all men (St. Matthew 5:16).

Perhaps at first, we may seem small and insignificant. But as we commit to the Kingdom of God, we mature, and our spiritual ascension in Christ begins. When the Potter is finished molding the clay, even the clay will know there has been a change! (Jeremiah 18:1-4).

It's not only your *Season*, it's your *Turn*… are you ready?

~ Pastor Michael Dean
Power City Ministries, Columbus, OH

Chapter 9
TRANSITIONING TO TRANSFORMATION

LIMINALITY: AN *Interval* BETWEEN

God does everything based on principles (rules, codes, or laws). God's law for planting is distinctly different from His law of harvesting. It is imperative to know which of God's laws are appropriate and applicable for your given situation or season. The principles for *trans*ition are governed by God's laws of movement. The principles for *transform*ation, however, are founded on God's rules concerning growth, maturity and developmental change. The wise King Solomon declared, "To everything there is a season, and a time to every purpose under the heaven" (Ecclesiastes 3:1). Knowing your season for accomplishing anything is critically important. Understanding the delicate balance between starting and stopping is as important as knowing the right season. Bestselling author, John Maxwell, addresses the subject of knowing the right season as, "The Law of Timing." In his book, The 21 Irrefutable Laws of Leadership, Maxwell states four classifications to timing:

1. Wrong action, wrong time equates to disaster
2. Wrong action, right time equates to mistake
3. Right action, wrong time equates to resistance
4. **Right action, right time equates to success**

Knowing the right time to plant will have a direct impact on the quantity and quality of production outcomes. Knowing the peak season to harvest what was planted is also important. Every planter should understand which precise tools are required for planting and harvesting. Utilizing the right tools in any given season equates to maximum success. Again, King Solomon, said, there is "A time to be born and a time to die, a time to plant and a time to harvest" (Ecclesiastes 3:2).

The wise king makes an interesting comparison. He makes an analogy between being born and dying to planting and harvesting. The analogous comparison helps to understand that there is a definite time for everything. Perhaps even more interesting is the metamorphosis between birth and death or planting and harvesting. The word "metaphor" is the root word of "metamorphosis" which comes from a Greek word meaning to transfer or carry across. Metaphors "carry" meaning from one word, image, or idea across to another (Nordquist, 2017, para.3). The word metamorphosis refers to the transformation that takes place in the dark night of the Christian soul and is derived from the New Testament (NT) Greek word for transformation *metamorphoo*.

Our Christian life-long journey is filled with metaphors of spiritual transformation. As NT believers, we are interested in experiencing an ongoing transformation. That is, we want to transition through a spiritual birth process that initiates a Christ–like growth and maturity. Every child of God desires growth, development and progress until "…we reach unity in the faith and in the knowledge of the Son of God and become mature, attaining to the whole measure of the fullness of Christ" (Ephesians 4:13). Each of us mature in specific ways like all other individuals, like some individuals, or perhaps, like no other individuals.

Often psychologists use the term "development" to mean a pattern of movement or continual transformation that begins at conception and continues through the entire life cycle. "Transformation" can be commonly defined, as a qualitative change in form, shape, or appearance. When status transformation occurs, i.e., people move from one relative position or standing in society to another relative position or standing that is a change. The pattern of change is, well, complicated. It involves several processes – biological, cognitive, social and even economical. Biology involves genes inherited from parents. Without surgical and cosmetic alterations biological changes are impossible. Cognitive processes involve individual thought, perception and language. Social processes involve relationships with other people, emotions and personality. Economics involves your financial state of being.

Changing any of the aforementioned, serves as a catalyst for grief, because grief is the conflicting feelings that come at the change in processes or patterns of behaviors. Rituals are stable social pathways of dealing with change in patterns of behaviors in day-to-day living (Neyrey, 1990, p.77):

- Uneducated people cross lines and become educated (*the ritual is graduation*)
- Single people cross lines and become husband and wife (*the ritual is* a *wedding*)
- Married people cross lines and become divorced (*the ritual is* a *divorce decree*)
- Legal people cross lines and become convicts (*the ritual is sentencing*)
- Sinful people cross lines and become purified (*the ritual is salvation*); and
- Living people cross lines and become dead (*the ritual is* a *funeral*)

With all rites of passage, there is also ambiguity, where we are not quite in one state or the other. Liminality is a term used in the study of anthropology (the study of humankind). Liminality (from the Latin word līmen, meaning "a threshold") is the uncertainty or disorientation that occurs in the transition from one state to another. Liminality occurs during rites of passage. There is a process of (1) Separation, (2) Liminality and finally, (3) Reincorporation. The term "rite of passage" was first used by the French anthropologist Arnold van Gennep, for any of the ceremonies which mark or ensure a person's transition from one status to another within society (The Chambers Dictionary, 2009).

Rites of passage are what Christians experience during life-long developmental learning. Rites of passage, which we are exploring in this chapter, are interconnected to transition and transformation. Transitioning from one phase of growth and development to another is representative of movement. Movement, however, does not equate to change of spiritual condition or mentality. Change is often resisted and not welcomed especially by those who feel absolutely no need for it. Change invokes anxiety and, in some instances, even hostility.

Transition without change is potentially dangerous. For example, godly conviction will draw sinners from bar stools to church pews. That represents transition, i.e., movement from an ungodly place to a sacred place. However, if there is no behavioral evidence of spiritual conversion, there has been transition but no change!

The sinner has transitioned from a bar stool to a church pew but remains unrepentant or unchanged. Change of venue does not equate to a change of heart. I'll share another example of transition without change. While working on my undergraduate degree, I conducted an empirical study on a newly built housing community. The housing units were beautifully designed. The landscaping was immaculate. It had the appearance of a development worthy of any upper middle-class community in the Mid-Western United States. Upon completion, the entire development was purchased by the U.S. Federal government. An initiative was enacted. This honorable and most noble project attempted to transition under-employed residents from a low-income zip code to the new housing units. The outcome was obvious. The new housing development looked like the old community within a matter of a few years. Because the new residents transitioned but there was no change in education, skills or income status. Whenever transition occurs it should always be accompanied with transformational change.

Rites of passage are status transformation rituals. When status transformation occurs, that is, people move from one relative position or standing in society to another relative position or standing – that represents a change. Again, change brings about instability in the dynamics of any human relationship or system. People are often unsure and perhaps even afraid of change. Change, therefore, brings about trepidation and grief. Grief is the direct result of conflicting feelings that often materialize whenever there is change in any normal pattern of behaviors. Unfortunately, Christians are not immune. Generally, we do not like change. Unless, of course, we are personally responsible for making changes that suit our preferences.

To further underscore the importance of transition and transformation, consider life's various phases of on-going development and rites of passage. Adolescence is a rite of passage from childhood to adulthood. In adolescence there is liminality. The adolescent is not quite a child and not quite an adult. For the child to become an emotionally healthy and mature adult, s/he must go through the adolescence phase. In this transition, the adolescent will face physical changes, sexual changes, values changes, moral changes, religious changes, struggles connected with independence, pressures to conform and innumerable relational conflicts.

Nevertheless, no adult can escape or bypass the liminality of adolescence. Everyone will deal with the psychological and physiological dynamics of adolescence differently. Some will sail through it, for their own unique reasons. Others will struggle horribly and never become a mature adult. For the remainder of their lives a familiar refrain will be heard, "Grow up!" This stinging verbal rebuke will serve as a continual reminder that they have not yet successfully navigated life's maturation continuum.

Anyone who wants to be a mature adult must traverse the space between childhood and adulthood called, adolescence. If it is navigated effectively, a transformation will take place that is imperceptible to the person. A mature adult will have transitioned from the dark nebulous night of adolescence into the spectacular morning light of adulthood – transition to transformation! Growth is imperceptible to the person undergoing transformative change. However, to everyone else, growth is glaringly apparent.

Prayerfully, your childhood was healthy enough for you to transition through the uncertainties of adolescence. Whether it was or not, you have two options: (1) Resist growing up and learn to live in ambiguity; or (2) learn to navigate life, as you lean on God's everlasting arm. There are no other options!

The next rite of passage is anniversaries or birthdays. An anniversary, such as a wedding anniversary, marks the passage of another year of marriage. Birthdays represent the passage of another year of life. Birthdays and anniversaries are times of liminality. An anniversary represents exiting the previous year and standing on the threshold of the coming year. The anniversary marks the status transformation and calls for celebration. People and institutions alike celebrate the fact that they transition from one year into the next. These milestones should also remind everyone that they are moving from one juncture to the next, from a less mature to a more mature period of existence.

Marital transformation is based on the same praxis as birthdays and anniversaries. Amazingly, most bible lecturers rarely teach the obviousness of this truth! Why do some singles think that marriage is going to be a Hollywood fairytale? They think this because they have not been taught about the transformational challenges associated with marriage. If two people married never have relational challenges at all, then I believe someone is either lying, in denial, or extraordinarily medicated!

The next rite of passage is grief. You may not think of grief as a rite of passage, because we have so much information on it that we have become numb or insensitive to the dynamism of the process. Grief is that liminality between having someone or something and experiencing some change with respect to that someone or something. In the case of death, for example, one moment you are fellowshipping with your mate, friend, or co-worker and in the next minute, they are physically gone, but not psychologically or emotionally grieved. Therefore, in a sense, the person is not gone. But because you haven't properly processed the loss, saying goodbye, and moving back into life in a healthy way without grieving will not be possible.

For me, saying goodbye to Mom was painful. Her transitioning was slow and complicated with health-related challenges. No reasonably intelligent person wants to see their loved one suffer. I knew passing away was eminent but resisted it. Chelly, however, was completely unexpected. Her transitioning was sudden, tragic and extremely difficult for me to date. Dad's passing was not as difficult because closure was attained. He and I were able to reconcile our differences. We were able to travel the coastal shores of Southern California and have therapeutic talk sessions for years. Tom witnessed my professional and academic achievements.

In other words, he saw what Mom and Chelly did not. In that respect, for me, Tom was the designated family ambassador. He sat on the sofa in my office after my promotion to CEO. He watched me receive a doctorate degree. Again, his being present at those milestones in my life was symbolic of Diane and Michelle's presence and more importantly, their joyous approval. So, Tom's transitioning was difficult but not devastating.

Grief is a process of living between the person's life and death. When we are in grief, the person is not alive or dead. They are still alive in many of our thoughts, memories, and habits, but physically no longer available. That absence is emotionally difficult especially during holidays, birthdays, anniversaries or the date of their transition.

Therefore, we must navigate through the liminality of grief if we are to come out into the bright light of new possibilities. No one escapes grief! Some people may not be cognizant of the emotions associated with their grief, but they cannot escape grief. No one knows how long the grief process will take! For some, days, weeks, or months are all that is required; however, for others, it might last for a year or more. If, however, we allow grief to have its place, a miraculous transformation will take place during liminality.

We will come out of the in-between interval better, not bitter! Weeping may last for a night, but joy arrives in the morning light. Afterwards, we will look forward instead of backward. We will hold on to unconflicted, wonderful memories, while being surprisingly open to the future!

But, thank God for the nights; because without those nights there would be no growth and no glorious mornings. In conclusion, liminality is experienced when a child of God is in between ending an experience, while preparing to begin a new one. Liminality is experienced between the early exuberance of early Christianity and learning how to have mature intimacy with Christ. There comes a time in every Saint's life when what was working during the early stages of Christianity is not happening as easily.

- Prayer doesn't seem to be as powerful
- Church doesn't seem to be as exciting
- Relationships seemingly lose their energy
- God seems to not answer as quickly or not at all

Many Christians drop out of the organized Church at this point and give up their spiritual disciplines. There are six spiritual disciplines that are pathways to more intimate fellowship with Jesus:

1. Bible reading and study
2. Prayer
3. Fellowship ("one another" relationships)
4. Witnessing (relationships with unbelievers)
5. Obedience to His Word
6. Meet *new* people, visit *new* places, read *new* books

These are often abandoned, because they don't seem to be working anymore. Is it possible that we were not doing these things because we valued relationship with Christ, but because we enjoyed how these activities made us *feel*? And when they no longer provided the enjoyment, they were abandoned, because we thought our spirituality was diminished or depleted? Let me take a moment and emphasize spiritual discipline six (6). If you always do what you've always done, you'll always get the same results! If you don't venture out of your concrete habitual routine, you will suffocate in boredom!

No spirit-filled born-again believer can mature without going through some dark and challenging soul searching! It is during those times that we learn to hold to God's unchanging hand, even in the dark! It becomes more about relationship and less about performance.

Positions in departments, boards and auxiliaries cease to be matters of organizational importance. Senseless competitions, fractions, divisions and endless arguments about who is the greatest in the congregation are performance related nonsense. Transformation or growth of any kind necessitates struggle, suffering, or pain of some kind! We need to stop fighting this pattern and learn to trust God in the uncertainty and darkness of liminality.

When our walk with Christ focuses on relationship and not performance through good works, maturity happens. It is in the struggle of the soul that we are transformed from performance-oriented, immature Saints to relationship-oriented, intimate worshippers of Jesus, the Christ. A metamorphosis occurs. We not only transition but there is recognizable change. That change signals to everyone that we have undergone a Christocentric transformation. This transformation will give our God the glory he deserves.

Chapter 10

Worship: The Healing Balm for the Soul

Wilt Thou *be* Made Whole?

There are many Christians who are still hurting from acts committed against them while they lived under the oppressive dominion of sin. Yes, it is difficult to believe but quite factual. Even after we have been delivered from sin, certain areas of our lives still need healing and require the attention of the Master Potter. Still not convinced? Then consider the emotional state of a person who has been successfully rescued from drowning: although completely rescued and quite safe, he may still have a phobia of water. Unless the Holy Spirit is permitted full access to the areas of our lives that require spiritual healing, we will continue to live in pain.

Sadly, many Christians do not believe in disciplining. They believe in absolute perfection at the moment of spiritual rebirth. If that were true, then the Lord would not have given "some apostles; and some prophets; and some evangelists; and some pastors and teachers for the perfecting of the saints, for the edifying of the body of Christ: till we all come in the unity of the faith, and of the knowledge of the Son of God, unto a perfect man, unto the measure of the stature of the fullness of Christ (Ephesians 4:11-13)."

According to the Ephesians (4:11-13), God has already provided everything needed to spiritually perfect (complete the disciplining process of) every born-again believer. So why is there still so much spiritual hurt and imperfection in us? Because either by words or deeds we have ignorantly professed to be sufficient of ourselves and capable of governing our lives without God's help! Or, in other rare cases, people have become content to live in spiritual pain, mental distress, and physical illness. Unfortunately, there are thousands of Christians comfortable, hiding in surrealism, pseudo testimonies, and blatant denial. They have been taught to believe "if I deny it, it will cease to exist." Wrong!

Olympic athletes will often insist on participating in their prospective events even when they have incurred serious injuries. They have mastered the science of ignoring pain. But pain is precious! It is our body's internal warning alarm system. The nervous system alerts the brain that something is malfunctioning. The internal alarm system will send an urgent message to the brain: cease walking immediately! Just imagine what would happen if you twisted your ankle but were unable to detect it. You would continue to perform your daily activities until stricken by paralysis because you were oblivious to the preciousness of pain.

The Holy Ghost is our spiritual alarm mechanism. He instantly informs us when something is spiritually malfunctioning. He rings the bell, blows the whistle, and flashes the red warning lights. Yet, we pretend not to hear Him, and I do mean pretend. Because His sheep not only hear, but in fact, know His voice (St. John 10:2-5).

The Good Shepherd loves His sheep. That is why He is so protective. He persistently stands at the "door" of our stubborn human will, knocking and pleading for an opportunity to perform spiritual bypass surgery on our mixed-up lives. The Master Surgeon bypasses our serious faults and deals directly with our critical needs! How long shall He be required to knock?

> *"Behold, I stand at the door, and knock: if any man hear my voice, and open the door, I will come in to him, and will sup with him, and he with me."*
>
> *~ Revelation 3: 20*

Beloved, it is time to be delivered from surrealism and denial. Stop pretending it never happened. I dare you to deal with it. All of it! Pull all the filthy hate, bitter resentment, and hidden shame linen out of the closet and stop hiding it. The stench of concealed regrets and the bitterness of guilt is destroying the lovely fragrance of your beautiful life. How long will you ignore the pain? Yet, thousands of Christians are still hostage to irrational fears and spiritually terrified by what might happen if they open up and allow the Lord to minister to that wounded area in their life. They are held hostage to "what-if-phobia!"

How many Christians really want a husband/wife but are afraid of developing a monogamous relationship because they have been hurt before? How many Christians really want physical healing, but have become dependent on a monthly disability check? They are actually more concerned about financial stability than being healed. What about sincere Christian pastoral leaders? According to David Kinnaman and The Barna Group's massive, three-year, in-depth research project entitled, The State of Pastors; only 10 percent of pastors surveyed prefer developing other leaders? Their main concern: what if the ministerial trainees succeed them in the pastorate?

How much time have you expended worrying about what–ifs? What if it does not happen? What if it's not successful? What if failure occurs? What if others find out about my past mistakes or lifestyle? Remember, we neither walk by sight (perception of existence), nor by what–ifs (what might happen), but we walk by faith (II Corinthians 5:7). Unfortunately, our minds are conditioned to respond more quickly to what-ifs rather than faith in the Word of God.

Earlier in this chapter, I referred to Christians who are still hurting from acts they committed or acts others committed against them while they were sinners. Well, there are also many faithful Christians who are hurting daily from evil acts that have occurred since becoming Christians. They have been wounded while working in the Master's vineyard and unless inner healing takes place; their spiritual growth process will be permanently stunted.

After nearly 30 years in the ministry, I am convinced that Christians are rendered ineffective or, in other words, lose their anointed influence because they are no longer capable of either expressing love or receiving an expression of love. Usually the first sign of a spiritually wounded Christian is ungratefulness. Refusing to acknowledge the wonderful things that God has done is an act of ungratefulness. God does not appreciate His spiritual bride (the church) being ungrateful.

When a man is unable to express love, his emotional state is in serious jeopardy. When a woman refuses to receive love, she emotionally ostracizes herself. Jesus taught: "By this shall all men know that ye are my disciples, if ye have love one to another" (John 13:35). It becomes incumbent upon the Church to demonstrate the act of genuine love one for another. We must educate unbelievers in the biblical science of loving our family, our community, our nation, our world.

Maybe now you can better understand the strategy of Satan. His twisted agenda includes a massive propagation of pseudo love. He has substituted biblical love for a convoluted version of love. Satan prefers bravado not humility; he loves to promote Hollywood macho men in lieu of prayerful God-fearing mighty men. Lucifer adores glamour queens who promote idolatry and flagrant immorality. But he despises chaste, affectionate, God-fearing women. Since the enemy cannot emulate real love; he has a perverted imitation called lust.

The Church, however, has been empowered and authorized to ensure that this diabolical scheme is exposed. We will expose his scheme by demonstrating love. First, we must demonstrate what the Greeks called agape love. Agape love is the love that is exhibited between God and man. It is superseded by no higher form of love.

Next, we must demonstrate Eros. Eros love is displayed between a man and woman in the union of marriage. Eros love in a marriage should reflect the love that Christ has for the Church. That is why the Holy Spirit instructed Paul to write: "Husbands love your wives, even as Christ also loved the church..." (Ephesians 5:25). Lastly, we must demonstrate Philia love (deep friendship). Philia love is brotherly love toward our neighbor, whomever that entails.

As Christian soldiers, we are not immune to some of life's struggles and difficulties. Although, we are on a mission to gospelize the world for Jesus; occasionally we are hurt while working to spread the Master's message. Sometimes we're wounded unintentionally, but there are times when the enemy will use anybody to harm us physically and spiritually: believer and/or unbeliever.

Remember the gates to the psyche (soul) are imagination, conscience, memory, reason, and affections (see chapter 3). When your ability to give and receive love is thwarted, it is primarily due to damage in one of these areas, and unless inner healing takes place you will constantly live in emotional turmoil.

So, don't deny the pain because the injury will only get worse. Thank God that there is a healing balm for your soul. The secret is learning how to apply a spiritual balm to the wounded area of your life.

What is balm? There are many definitions for the word "balm." Webster's New World Dictionary (11ᵗʰ ed.) defines it as "a fragrant oil for healing or anointing. Anything that is healing or soothing, especially to the mind." We will focus on being healed and delivered; forget being soothed. If all you desire is a physical soothing, then go squeeze a little Ben-Gay on your body and rub it in. Perhaps the physical ache will stop, but your heartache won't! But, if you have had enough of the pain, then get in the healing position and prepare to be blessed.

God can heal you instantaneously or through a process of time. It is His choice. Don't be overly concerned about how long the healing process takes. It really does not matter what means God uses to heal you. The Potter knows exactly how to fix a broken vessel.

> *"And we know that all things work together for good to them that love God, to them who are the called according to His purpose."*
>
> *~ Romans 8:28*

God's healing balm was never more critically needed than during my tenure of employment with an internationally known Christian retailing company. The disappointment experienced during that time was unbelievable. However, during that ten-month period, the Master Potter gave me a greater understanding of how all things "fit" together for them that love Him. Understanding this principal is critically important to every born-again believer.

King Solomon admonished us: "Wisdom is the principal thing; therefore, get wisdom: and with all thy getting get understanding" (Proverbs 4:7). Understanding means knowing everything that happens to you is not good, but that all things work together for good. Understanding this principal will help you remain spiritually anchored while riding through the storms of life. The Living Bible Paraphrased says:

> *"And we know that all that happens to us is working for our good if we love God and are fitting into His plans."*
>
> *~ Romans 8:28*

Many Christians perpetuate the falsehood that once you are saved nothing awful will happen to you. But the Word of God does not teach that Christians are immune to trouble. How can spiritual warriors avoid warfare? We were born to conquer! Of course, there are times during battle, or even in preparation for a battle, when we are wounded. That is why the Master Potter provided balm!

BROKEN *to be* MADE WHOLE

The first couple of weeks as sales administrator were terrific. My first day consisted of getting acquainted with company protocol. This was not merely a business. It was a ministry that operated in a business format. Each week began with corporate devotions that included singing, teaching, testimonials and ended with prayer. It was quite fascinating to watch the president, vice-president and senior managers of a multi-million-dollar company sit in a huge circle asking God for guidance.

During the first month of my employment. Megan, our key accounts/Christian Booksellers Association (CBA) sales manager resigned from her CBA sales manager's position. She informed me that she no longer desired to perform dual roles. She had decided to concentrate on one area. Besides, her real desire, as she put it, was to "spend more time with my family." When she told me of her resignation, I slowly sat down in my chair, turned toward the window and stared outside.

After a few moments of silence, we began to discuss the details of her resignation. During our discussion it became quite apparent that this was a well-planned decision and not just a knee-jerk reaction to something.

Megan was very confident that company sales would not suffer. Nevertheless, there remained one unresolved question that sorely needed to be answered in my mind: "Who is going to manage the daily operations of the sales department?" My facial expressions must have asked the question before I was able to verbalize the thought. "I have already mentioned your name to the president." She continued, "I've asked him to consider you for the position of sales manager."

Being a seasoned professional, I was not easily excited by lofty promises to "drop my name to the corporate brass." My previous experiences with ambitious middle managers made me very leery of them. All too often their agenda included searching for innovative ways that involved "stepping on the shoulders" of anyone, especially their peers. This crab-in-the-barrel technique was necessary to climb the corporate ladder to senior manager status.

Therefore, when dealing with these corporate crabs, my actions were governed by a simple but effective philosophy: Trust them at your own risk! If someone was attempting to do me a favor there must be a hidden agenda. Besides, new employees usually remained relatively unknown in big companies. They are often referred to as the new person in sales, what's-his-face from accounting, or what–ya–ma–call–it in advertising. I wanted concrete assurance that serious consideration would be given to me regarding the CBA sales manager's position.

Unfortunately, no immediate assurance would be forthcoming. A massive corporate reorganization took place and a new national sales manager's (NSM) position was created. Emily was selected and promoted from within the secular market division. Our company president, who was also chief executive officer (CEO) gave the new national sales manager carte blanche. If there was going to be another CBA sales manager, it would be Emily's decision.

Several weeks passed by and there were no new job postings nor any official information about a CBA sales manager's position. It was now well into the Christmas holiday season and our sales department was in crucial need of leadership. One day Megan approached me and asked, "Has anyone said anything to you about the position?" "No, not yet, I said."

She continued, "Several times we (Emily and the president) have discussed this. Each time I have asked them to at least give you a decision." This time Megan's sincerity was overwhelmingly believable. Believable enough to disregard my own rule and trust a corporate scribe. This was my mistake.

Now my curiosity was demanding some answers. Immediately after the company Christmas dinner I approached Emily and asked to speak with her regarding the decision to find a new sales manager. Emily informed me that her plans certainly included hiring another CBA sales manager. My professional portfolio was promptly placed in her hand.

The next week Emily came into my office. We began to discuss her vision for the sales department. My instinctive reaction was that this discussion was not just chit–chat. It felt more like an informal interview. After nearly an hour of "bouncing thoughts off each other," we concluded. Emily commented that there was really no need for her to conduct a formal interview. She liked what she heard "I'd like to get you started as soon as possible." However, the company president insisted on having all candidates for CBA sales manager interviewed by a private consultant. This notable consultant would not be available until the first week in January.

My interview with the private consultant was intense but not very long. I had mixed feelings regarding my performance. Two weeks passed and not one word was mentioned about the results of my interview. I kept wondering, why doesn't someone keep me abreast of what's going on? Apparently, our department had a history of not effectively communicating. It was not uncommon to see sales personnel quite irritated by not having sufficient information to properly service their accounts. There was a definite need to improve communications.

Finally, I decided to approach Emily about the results of the interview and status of the position. She apologized for not keeping me abreast. Emily told me that when Ms. Abramovich, the consultant debriefed the president she commented: "He'll require some specialized technique training, but if he is only half as good as he seems, he'll be excellent."

"Does this mean that the job is mine or have you considered other candidates?" I asked. She said, "No, you're the only candidate. I am just waiting for the president to give his approval." Approval? That statement did not agree with my spirit. As a matter of fact, it made me skeptical and suspicious. Because I personally overheard the president say just the opposite. Perhaps there was something transpiring that Emily was unwilling to share with me. Her "just waiting for the president" was too generic and there was hesitation in her voice.

Something else was delaying her decision. "How soon before you meet with the president to discuss a starting date," I asked. Emily assured me that it would be real soon. However, she still neglected to provide a specific date.

This behavior was totally uncharacteristic of Emily. Her managerial acumen was well known throughout the company. Her ability to access information and be decisive warranted the promotion to national sales manager. Several weeks went by and my anxieties festered. Finally, I approached her about the status of the position. "Where are you with the CBA Manager's position?" I asked. Emily responded by explaining her reservations about turning the department over to someone before the staff "really had a chance to get to know her." Huh? Of course, she had a perfectly contrived explanation. You see, Emily wanted to train each person to ensure all employees were aware of her professional expectations. Emily promised, however, that all responsibilities of managing the sales department would be mine effective the first day of March. Strangely, there was a vague sense of disbelief. Why couldn't I believe her answer was sincere?

Try to imagine how difficult it was for me coming to work the next forty-five days. Emily never discussed the sales department with me and there weren't any training strategies developed. However, once she stated plans were being made to send me to a specialized sales training seminar. This was supposed to happen before March, but it did not. A barrage of questions began tumbling over in my mind. Of course, the adversary was right there adding doubts: "Why don't you get out of here. They really don't like you. Why are you the only Black male in the entire corporation?" Yes, I dealt with this mental anguish every day!

The enemy was constantly reminding me of what I had left behind: a decent salary, a huge downtown office, et cetera, et cetera, et cetera. A voice kept asking: Why are you here? What are you doing? Why are you allowing these euro-centric people to play games with your career?

In a unique way, God was hiding Himself in what seemed to be a dilemma. Many people were being ministered to. Co-workers were coming to me for counseling and prayer. People were asking questions about the deity of Jesus. I found myself praying for the birth of ministries. Although, professionally disenchanted, it was strangely wonderful to be in a professional environment where employees openly asked questions about Jesus.

This was incredible. God in His infinite wisdom meticulously placed people together in this company who otherwise would have never met. These events could not be dismissed as merely happenstance. Many people had grown weary of the confines of traditionalism. They were weary of religious platitudes and formalities. It was obvious that God was using me to improve relationships and strengthen ministries.

Finally, March arrived, albeit there was no sense of elation about starting in a new position. None of the promises regarding specialized training had been kept. For those reasons and many others, I was not surprised by the unusual meeting that took place at the start of our work day. Emily informed me that there would be yet another delay. "The sales staff needs more time to get used to me being their leader." Emily continued, but her words were like tinkling cymbals. Her reasons for not keeping me abreast of her intentions were simply inexcusable.

She also stated that the entire sales department would be renovated to accommodate additional personnel and a supervisor. This renovation had already been approved. Immediately after the renovation, the company would be purchasing new furniture for our department. And lastly, she promised: I would be placed in a new training status that would include a salary increase and last for 60 days only. Effective the first day of May, "it will be yours."

The only reason I didn't resign was due to Emily's comments made the next day at our weekly staff meeting. She informed the entire sales staff that they must bring all personnel and work-related matters to me whenever she was unavailable. Next, Emily and I spent hours discussing future strategies relating to further development of the sales department. We also decided that it was in the company's best interest for me to attend the international CBA convention in Anaheim, CA. My wife was also approved to travel with me.

Also, during the month of March, Emily, two of the sales representatives and I traveled to Tampa, Florida to a retailer's international trade show. I personally traveled and stayed with the company president. While in Tampa, I was introduced to corporate buyers and other company CEO's (as part of the managerial training).

After returning from Tampa the training continued. By mid-April, I had visited most of our major accounts, worked in production, and was familiar with customer service, and accounting procedures. Toward the end of April, Emily was required to visit one of our major secular gift accounts located in Utah. Once again, I performed as acting sales manager in her absence. Although, I never informed anyone, it was obvious to most: I was going to become the next CBA sales manager. Several employees asked me: "When are we going to get another CBA manager?" My canned reply: "Soon…I hope."

When Emily returned from Utah, our professional interaction was minimal. She seemed distanced. It was as if she purposely avoided me. Concerned, I requested a meeting. We met at the break table in the warehouse. The interpersonal chemistry was discomfiting and disturbing. There was limited eye contact – another bad sign. We talked about the success of her trip and departmental issues that required her immediate attention. Before the meeting ended, I asked this question: "Is everything still on schedule to take place in May?" Emily replied, "Yes sir, everything is still on schedule."

The following Friday, on April 19, Emily came in my office and shut the door behind her. She said: "I want to give you an update on the job situation." She continued, "I have been trying to think of a way to tell you. We have…decided to go with someone else." Déjà vu!

While calmly sitting there, staring out of the window, many thoughts went through my mind. Foremost was the incredible fact that God had prepared me for this moment. Unable to get angry, I said: "perhaps it was not meant for me to have this job." Emily kept talking but the Holy Ghost whisked my mind back to October 24, 1995. Evangelist Naomi Sessley prayed for me that day. In her prophetic prayer she said: "God we know that promotion neither comes from the east or the west but from you."

Cognizant again of Emily's voice, I heard: "You certainly have demonstrated a Christian spirit." My reply was: "Thank you," and with those words the meeting ended. There was no denying my disappointment. Even after arriving home, that sense of disappointment lingered in my soul. Of course, I was disappointed, especially since planning to travel to Anaheim. That evening my soul was restless.

Early the next morning before sunrise, Almar, Ashley, and my wife traveled to Cincinnati for a soccer tournament. Phillip remained with me. I was scheduled to teach at a Worship Arts Conference in Columbus and serve as the keynote speaker for a pastoral anniversary in Toledo, Ohio, the very next day. That morning there were many questions reverberating in my mind. Lord, why was it necessary for me to go through this agonizing experience? What purpose does this serve? Why must I constantly be humiliated in this town? As I lay there, tears filled my eyes. A wrestling match in my soul ensued between anger and forgiveness.

Emotionally exhausted, I finally concluded my anger wasn't about a position with any company. It was about being intentionally lied too, purposely misused, and feeling violated by church-going folk. Yes, tears were staining my pillow but they were tears of hurt, anger, embarrassment and resentment. Now it was distinctly clear why so many people simply have no respect for folk who call themselves Christians.

My feelings of anger were abruptly interrupted by the same hideous hellish snickering last heard while standing in the unemployment line. Evil seemingly always comes on cue. It comes at your lowest ebb or weakest moment to tempt, taunt or mock you. Without hesitating, those spirits were rebuked in Jesus name! Then, in the silence of that moment, the Lord asked me a question. "Do you not think that Joseph was hurt when he was imprisoned?" Immediately the anger subsided, but only for a brief season.

Later that morning Elder Eric Colter arrived from Dayton. We decided to go to the conference early. Our departing early was also a part of God's divine plan. God was gracious enough to allow me not to be home when the conference director called to notify me of a schedule change. By the time we arrived my teaching time had elapsed. Evangelist Johanna Towns was teaching in the time slot that had been rescheduled for me.

We sat in the back of the chapel. It was as if she had prepared the class specifically for me. Her topic was "Healing the broken-hearted through worship." She dealt with the dangers of proceeding while pretending! "Many Christians are destroyed for a lack of knowledge (Hosea 4:6). They simply have never been taught how to get to the rudiments of their pain," she said. Although my soul was still hurting, the Lord was healing me.

Nevertheless, my testimony was not quite ready to include "forgive them Lord, for they know not what they did". The evening worship service afforded me an opportunity to begin dealing with a very deep wound.

Our sagacious guest speaker was Bishop Norman L. Wagner, my spiritual father in the gospel. His message was, "Taking it to the next level." One of the statements Bishop Wagner made that evening was very difficult for me to accept. He said: "God has not completed the work in you. Therefore, you must go back to that job."

Upon hearing that statement my body snapped to a rigid military sitting position. "What did he say?" That same question kept repeating itself in my head like an old badly scratched compact disc. "What did he say?" "What did he really say?" "Did he say, Go back?" I thought: "Bishop, my name is not mule! I am not taking another kickin'!"

It was hard enough just dealing with the whole concept of forgiving, let alone going back for another helping of "in yo' face!" Forget it! There was absolutely nothing, in my opinion, worth going back to. Furthermore, the interpersonal chemistry and professional climate simply would never be the same.

We arrived back home around 1:00 a.m. My spirit was restless. Two of the Psalms were burning in my heart, "O spare me, that I may recover strength, before I go hence and be no more" (Psalm 39:13). "I waited patiently for the Lord; and he inclined unto me, and heard my cry. He brought me up also out of a horrible pit, out of the miry clay, and set my feet upon a rock, and established my goings" (Psalm 40:1-2).

Eventually, overcome by fatigue, I fell asleep. In the morning we traveled to Toledo, Ohio. God blessed us with a wonderfully anointed service. Elder Colter drove Phillip and me back to Columbus, and he returned to Dayton. The necessary mental preparation to return to work began. I simply could not deny what God said through Bishop Wagner.

Hiding pain was not my forte. Just thinking about returning to that environment created vexation in my soul. How could we sit in close proximity during devotions as if nothing ever occurred? For nearly an hour I tried to dismiss my feelings as an overreaction to an innocent business decision. But deep down inside I knew differently.

My soul was hemorrhaging. Hemorrhaging is the worst type of bleeding because it occurs internally. You can sing in the choir, organize the conference, and preach the text while hemorrhaging to death!

Worst of all, my wound did not happen in a nightclub or a crack house. It occurred while working in the Master's vineyard. Yes, it happened while in the house of a friend!

In retrospect, the next month of my life really misrepresented Jesus because it lacked authentic love and commitment to anything or anyone. My behavior was purely mechanical. It lacked passion. Even when the hurt began to subside, anger immediately took its place. Every day was a major mental warfare. Going to work was extremely difficult and even being at home didn't help. Regardless of the location, anger reigned inside my soul. All my knowledge of God was useless because I was too angry to apply it. For that reason, King Solomon warned, "Be not hasty in thy spirit to anger: for anger resteth in the bosom of fools" (Ecclesiastes 7:9).

Every important facet of my life was affected: marriage, ministry, and fatherhood. In acknowledgement of my desperate need of God's intervention, I got on the floor prostrate and prayed. My soul was in danger of being consumed by wrath.

That day I allowed the Holy Spirit to access the secret closet of my soul. He ministered to me and everything finally came out. I had an audience with God and took full advantage of it. For the first time in weeks I was able to verbalize my anger and resentment. It was a deep resentment and God knew it! It was more than not getting a job. I found out that Emily and other senior managers were privately negotiating with another person while continuing to make promises to me. Their conniving affected my family's quality of life and that was a serious offense!

However, the Lord did not address what they did. He kept dealing with me about purpose and then He said, "I will not curse this company. I will bless it." That statement gave me insight and new direction. If I wanted God's favor, it was necessary to bless whomever He was blessing! I'd played the role of Balaam once before. Now, it was time to succeed from the memory of failure. At once my heart changed! The next twenty minutes were spent blessing every department in that company along with Emily, the president and anyone else that came to mind. I didn't say it was easy. Anyone who says that loving folk who don't love you is easy; obviously has never tried to do it. Nevertheless, after praying, the spirit of hatred no longer tormented me. That victory was desperately needed. The issues of hurt and anger had been buried in the blood of Jesus.

The peace of God was resting in my heart now. It was a long time coming but a change had indeed come. Of course, returning to work required me to have a tough-as-steel mentality because the renovation project was complete and, as previously planned, new furniture was purchased. There were, however, a few additional changes. These new changes included: my cherry wood desk being taken and given to Emily's assistant, my computer being taken and given to someone in marketing, and finally, Emily decided that I no longer needed a telephone. Jesus!

She did, however, diplomatically offer me the opportunity to select a new desk from all the old desks that had been stored in the company warehouse; my choice, of course. Determined not to subscribe to Murphy's Law, I decided to take King Solomon's advice by not allowing my mouth to cause my flesh to sin (Ecclesiastes 5:6).

The events of this day were merely a challenge to the testimony of my deliverance from the shackles of anger. So, when the movers were instructed to place my metal desk in Emily's office facing a wall, I did not get angry. Yet, despite of all this, God said stay. But my spiritual instincts knew it would not be for much longer.

After the renovation, my work days usually began like this; I'd come to work, go sit in the utility room (because I refused to sit in Emily's queendom and stare at the wall), and run statistical reports. The utility room was a small walk–in closet sized room that consisted of a copier, fax machine and postage equipment. It was quite embarrassing. People kept asking: "Where is your office?" What should have been obvious was not. Have you ever had the need to express your feelings but couldn't find a listener? Deep inside, every human being has a burning desire to be heard. Often citizen riots, company mayhems and government coup d'état are merely a reflection of people not being heard. Helping a hurting person to verbalize and express internal struggles has invaluable therapeutic benefits! Receive that.

Every day brought another heaping helping of humiliation, and regardless of the countless times I quoted, "Not that I speak in respect of want: for I have learned, in whatsoever state I am, therewith to be content (Philippians 4:11)," the situation was no less embarrassing. Why was there such an intense struggle, continual embarrassment and professional debilitation? God's purpose in all this was nebulous to me. But I knew the Master Builder was reshaping me.

"Behold, I go forward, but he is not there; and backward, but I cannot perceive him: On the left hand, where he doth work, but I cannot behold him: he hideth himself on the right hand, that I cannot see him: But he knoweth the way that I take: when He hath tried me, I shall come forth as gold."

~ Job

One Tuesday morning, while still in bed, the mere thought of traveling forty-five minutes one way to sit in a utility room and perform "keep him busy

Purpose Guided Passion

Your professional occupation and divine purpose are not necessarily synonymous.

work" created a burden in my soul. As I sat up and put my feet on the floor, tears began uncontrollably running down my grief-stricken face. "Lord, please help me, Jesus." Unable to get relief from this oppressive grief, I felt led to call my pastor. He listened attentively to the sporadic details of the past few months of my life. For nearly twenty minutes I updated him on the debasing events of the past sixty days. Now and then I'd say: "Pastor?" He reassuringly responded: "I'm still here." Confident he was listening, I continued. Pastor's eventual responses poignantly reassured me that God was still in control of everything, despite of all that had occurred. He neither attempted to mollify me nor mitigate the severity of my concerns. In fact, he stated: "Considering all that you have been through, your behavior is not in any way atypical or abnormal."

As the sermon was being preached, the Holy Ghost revealed to me that professional occupation and divine purpose are not synonymous. Paul by trade/profession was a tent maker (Acts 18:1-3), but God called him (divine purpose) to be an Apostle (Galatians 1:1). The Lord changed seventeen years of secular thinking in that moment. My previous anti-biblical thinking was formed by a societal belief: "Your occupation defines who and what you are."

Please don't take heed to every name people call you. Those names will not always rightly identify you. Some have called me inept, ugly, loser, and even worse, but Jesus called me: His son! That is what I am by spiritual rebirth; a son of the Most High God. What difference does it make if your occupation is a custodian, chef, or chemist? "And whatsoever we do in word or deed, do all in the name of the Lord Jesus, giving thanks to God and the Father by Him (Colossians 3:17).

In the closing moments of our conversation pastor prayed for me. When he rebuked the spirit of depression; the burden and grief associated with it immediately departed. With the words, "Glenn, be encouraged," our dialogue ended. Slowly placing the phone down, I stood up, stretched my arms toward heaven and worshipped Jesus. The Lord delivered, healed, and restored me with His love and spiritual balm.

In the Old Testament balm was an odoriferous substance used for medicinal purposes and applied to external wounds (Jeremiah 8:22; 46:11; 51:8). The spiritual balm, however, is used explicitly for internal wounds. Spiritual balm is not magical hocus-pocus dust! The balm is comprised of God's holy anointing mixed with pure worship, i.e., your willingness to submit to His will. This spiritual salve will heal and restore the deepest of wounds, even if you are wounded while in the house of a friend!

It took God's anointing to break the yoke of resentment, hurt, hatred and depression. Worship, however, kept all the residual out of my soul and spirit! My willingness to forgive, coupled with faith in God, made it possible for me to continue my life. Indeed, restoration had finally come. Now, the word empathy was merely no longer a sociological term. I can discern the silent pain behind my brother's and sister's smile.

I know both how to be abased, and I know how to abound: everywhere and in all things, I am instructed both to be full and hungry, both to abound and to suffer need. I can do all things through Christ which strengtheneth me.

~ A Son of God

Chapter 11

JESUS THE ULTIMATE WORSHIPPER

PERFORMING *the* WILL OF GOD

Jesus was the Ultimate Worshipper. He was preoccupied with doing the will of his Father (St. Luke 2:49). When the disciples asked their Master to teach them how to pray, Jesus' response was categorical: He praised the Father, He worshipped the Father, and He prayed to the Father (St. Luke 11:1).

Consider the key components of the "model prayer." Jesus' statement consists of Jesus' praise to the Father: "Our Father which art in heaven, hallowed be thy name." Praise is an act of devotion and adoration. Jesus' statement also reveals the residence of the Father; the Father rules every dimension from heaven. Then, Jesus blesses His Father's name because it is sacred and holy.

Secondly, Jesus teaches through prayer the critical importance of worship. "Thy Kingdom come. Thy *will* be done in earth, as it is in heaven." Jesus prayed for the heavenly Father's *will* to be done. This statement contains the ingredients of submission, willingness, and total surrender. This statement acknowledges the eternal sovereignty of God and the absolute perfection of His divine *will*.

The third category of Jesus' prayer makes requests: "Give us this day our daily bread And lead us not into temptation, but deliver us from evil." Notice, our Savior did not make any requests until He praised and worshipped the Father. It is ridiculous to expect blessings from a God we will not praise and worship. Remember, praise is an act of devotion and adoration. Worship is acknowledging the sovereignty and Lordship of Jesus in every facet of our life.

The Master's prayer set precedence for all New Covenant worshippers! Jesus immediately recognized the sovereignty of the Father and the absolute necessity of obeying the Father's *will* above everything and everyone. Jesus' priority was to bless the Father regardless of what the Father did or did not perform, and immediately after blessing the Father, Jesus proclaimed: "Thy *will* be done."

Jesus demonstrated clarity of direction. He knew the Father's divine purpose for His life. Even when His flesh desired to be spared, Christ prayed: "Father, if thou be *willing*, remove this cup from me: Nevertheless *not my will*, but thine (*His Father's will*), *be done*" (St. Luke 22:42). He preferred the perfect will of the Heavenly Father above His own! That's worship! And finally, when He died on the cross, Jesus said: "It is finished" (St. John 19:30).

The perfect will of God for His earthly life was finished. He performed the perfect will of God and lived a lifestyle of worship. Jesus left this testimony: I am a truthful and unselfish worshipper!

He constantly sought the will of the Father, not His own. When the Father chose not to deliver His Son from the cross, the Son still acknowledged the perfect will of the Father: Christ denied Himself and remained on the cross. Jesus' sacrifice was the ultimate act of worship! Christ's example again proves that worship requires a surrendered will.

If Jesus had prayed to be removed from the cross, angels would have removed Him. However, Jesus chose to fulfill the Father's purpose by placing the Father's will above His own. Remember, worship does not make any requests of God, but in fact, acknowledges God's awesome supremacy and sovereignty. No single act proves this point more than Jesus' sacrifice on Calvary. Jesus proved to be the New Testament's Ultimate Worshipper (Revelation 1:8; 17-18)! Amen.

References

James, John. W. & Friedman, Russell. 2009. *The grief recovery handbook: The action*
    program for moving beyond death, divorce, and other losses including health, career, and faith. New York, NY: William Morrow, pages 43-44.

Johnson, Joey. 2016. *Grief: A biblical pathway to God.* Dallas, TX: St. Paul Press, page 65.
    Sermonic notes used by permission. Bishop Josephus Johnson II sermon "*The*
    Metaphors of Metamorphosis: Rites of passage 2".

Kushner, Harold. S. 1981. *When bad things happen to good people.* New York, NY:
    Schocken Books, pages 46-47.

Maxwell, John C. 2007. The 21 irrefutable laws of leadership. Nashville, TN: Thomas
    Nelson, pages 196-198.

MERRIAM-WEBSTER'S DICTIONARY (11th ed.). 2003. Springfield, MA: Merriam-Webster Inc.

NASB "Scripture quotations taken from the New American Standard Bible® (NASB),
    Copyright © 1960, 1962, 1963, 1968, 1971, 1972, 1973, 1975, 1977, 1995 by The Lockman Foundation Used by permission. www.Lockman.org"

Neyrey, Jerome H.1990. *Paul in other words: A cultural reading of his letters* (p.77).
    Louisville, Kentucky: Westminster/John Knox Press.

Nordquist, Richard. 2017, March 3. *What is a metaphor?* Retrieved March 22, 2017, from
    https://www.thoughtco.com/what-is-a-metaphor-1691773

Santrock, John W. 1989. *Life-span development* (3rd ed.).
Dubuque, IA: Wm. C. Brown.
Smith, James K. A. 2016. *You are what you love: The spiritual power of habit*. Grand
        Rapids, MI: Brazos Press.

The Chambers Dictionary (11th ed.). 2009. Crescent, Edinburgh:
Chambers Harrap
        Publishers Ltd.

The Living Bible Paraphrased copyright © 1971 by Tyndale
House Foundation. Used by
        permission. Carol Stream, Illinois: Tyndale House
Publishers Inc. *Psalm 75:6.*

Vine, William E. 1986. *An Expository Dictionary of Biblical Words*. Nashville, TN: Thomas
        Nelson.

Walker, Clarence. 1992. *Biblical Counseling with African Americans: Taking a Ride in the*
        Ethiopians Chariot. Grand Rapids, MI: Zondervan
Publishing House.

Wright, H. Norman. 2011. *The complete guide to crisis & trauma counseling: What to do*
        and say when it matters most! Ventura, CA: From Gospel
Light, pages 144-155.

Zodhiates, Spiros (Editor). 1993. *The complete word study New Testament (word study*
        series). Chattanooga, TN: AMG.

SPECIAL ACKNOWLEDGEMENTS

Walter-Robinson Families

Leadership Training Consultants Staff CA/OH

Church of Christ of the Apostolic Faith

Trinity Lutheran Seminary, OH

Michael Morbitzer

Professor Patricia Brown

Professor Dr. Kevin Dudley

Rev. Dr. Lynn Nakamura

Bishop F. Josephus Johnson

House of the Lord Ministries, OH

Mildred Penn

Patsy Sigers & Family

Gwen Lewis

Claystone Press Photography- (Rear Photo)